INSIDE
Ferrari

Michael Dregni

Motorbooks International
Publishers & Wholesalers

To my wife and friend, Sigrid Ann Arnott

First published in 1990 by Motorbooks International Publishers & Wholesalers, P O Box 2, 729 Prospect Avenue, Osceola, WI 54020 USA

© Michael Dregni, 1990

Motorbooks International is a certified trademark, registered with the United States Patent Office

The information in this book is true and complete to the best of our knowledge. All recommendations are made without any guarantee on the part of the author or publisher, who also disclaim any liability incurred in connection with the use of this data or specific details

We recognize that some words, model names and designations, for example, mentioned herein are the property of the trademark holder. We use them for identification purposes only. This is not an official publication

Motorbooks International books are also available at discounts in bulk quantity for industrial or sales-promotional use. For details write to Special Sales Manager at the Publisher's address

Library of Congress Cataloging-in-Publication Data
Dregni, Michael.
    Inside Ferrari / Michael Dregni.
       p.   cm.
    Includes index.
    ISBN 0-87938-429-8 (hard)
    1. Ferrari automobile—Design and construction—History.
  I. Title.
  TL215.F47D74 1990   90-36303
  629.222'2—dc20   CIP

Printed and bound in Hong Kong

On the front cover: The 1954 Ferrari 375 Mille Miglia, serial number 0412AM, owned by Horace Jeffries of Orange, California. Jeffries purchased the car from actor William Holden and promptly drove it to the Bonneville Slat Flats for a 165 mph run. Since then, the Pinin Farina-bodied spyder has returned to race in the revival of its namesake, the Mille Miglia, on two occasions. The car is maintained by Francorchamps of America, Inc., of Newport Beach, California. *Randy Leffingwell*

Inset on the front cover: A rare look inside the Ferrari race shop in 1956–57. Workers assemble a 290 Mille Miglia sports racer. *Jesse Alexander*

On the back cover: The beginning of the assembly line for the limited-run Ferrari F40 at the Maranello factory in 1989. The chassis-body package had arrived from Scaglietti in Modena and was painted at the Ferrari paint shop before being wheeled atop a dolly to the assembly line.

On the frontispiece: A line of Ferrari F40s belonging to members of the factory-sponsored Ferrari Club Italia. The F40s were a small part of the collection of Ferraris at a club meet at the Grossetto, Italy, military airfield in 1989.

On the title page: A line of F40s parked down an alleyway between factory buildings at Maranello. The shipment of headlamps for the F40s was tardy, so the partially finished cars had been parked out of the way waiting to be completed and gathering dust in the meantime.

On the introduction pages: This way to Ferrari. The lighted sign of the prancing horse at the rear gate of the factory on via Musso in Maranello. Maranello village limits, and a race-prepped F40 arriving on transporter.

Contents

Acknowledgments

Many people have aided me in the compiling and writing of this book—some knowingly, others unwittingly.

I offer my thanks first to Dottore Luca Matteoni and Brenda Vernor of Ferrari S.p.A. for their assistance in making this project possible.

I also thank these people on the other side of the walls: Hilary A. Raab, Jr., for his enthusiasm, knowledge and generosity; Mark Wallach and Bob Wallace for their time in recounting remembrances; Jesse Alexander for his hospitality and photographs; Phil Hill; Robert Bodin for his input and energy; Otis Meyer of *Road & Track* and Tim Blank of *Automobile Quarterly* for their research work; Dean Batchelor for his reading of the manuscript and for the sidebars on proprietary parts, valve springs and model identification.

Others to whom I owe thanks include Craig Morningstar of Alfa Romeo; Giorgio Nada for advice and assistance; Mario Capitani, director of the Museo dell'Automobile Carlo Biscaretti di Ruffia; John Lamm and Randy Leffingwell for their technical advice; Stanley Nowak; John W. Barnes, Jr., of *Cavallino;* Lowell Paddock; T.E. Warth, Esq., for the trusted loan of books; Ed Niles; Scott Grundfor and Andre De Stepfanis of Scott Restorations; John Ling.

And then there are those who helped me unwittingly: I thank Angelo Parrilla for hospitality and assistance; Bruno Baccari for hospitality, friendship and enthusiasm in related matters; Paolo Giuri; Luigi Rivola for introducing me to the cardinal for the Vatican's foreign affairs.

Above all, my thanks and gratitude go to three others instrumental in making this project happen:

Lucia Reardon worked with me as translator; her dedication, enthusiasm, spirit and friendship are invaluable.

Elisa Campani of Ferrari S.p.A. guided me through the factories at Maranello and Modena; her patience, time and assistance have been priceless.

And finally, my wife, Sigrid Arnott, offered her usual wisdom, advice, interest and humor to the project.

One final note: I have tried to make contact to clear copyright on all historic photographs used here. Some were originally taken in the 1940s and were discovered in photo files or collections forty years later and on the other side of the Atlantic. If I have used an unmarked print without realizing its true origin, I offer my apologies.

Photographic Notes

For the photographs of the Ferrari and Scaglietti factories shot in 1989, the films used were Kodachrome 200 and Tri-X 400 black and white. The pictures were taken with a Nikon F2 with drive and a 20 mm or 35 mm lens. The camera, drive and battery pack were mounted on a monopod at all times. Natural light was used for the photos, except for the pictures within the foundry, where a small fill flash was added.

Preface

In examining a work of art—whether it be a Modigliani or a Ferrari—the creative process is as fascinating as the art itself. The story of the artist's life, the expression of genius and inspiration, the engineering of form and function all require an understanding for one to appreciate the finished piece.

Ferrari automobiles wear the badge and name of one man, but building those cars has been the work of many people. Enzo Ferrari was a great organizer and leader, and through the years he collected around himself teams of engineers, mechanics and drivers that reached greater heights than any of the individuals could have reached on his or her own. Each person involved in constructing Ferrari automobiles has played a part in shaping the cars, whether it be through design ideas, engineering solutions, hands-on mechanical innovations, a blueprint for a V–12 engine or a hammer's imprint in an aluminum body panel.

In this book, I have looked inside the factory, the race works, the *carrozzerie,* or bodyshops, and the component suppliers to examine how Ferrari automobiles have been engineered and constructed from the beginning of Scuderia Ferrari in 1929 to the founding of Ferrari Automobili and up to the Ferrari factory of 1990.

In 1946–47, Ferrari's first Tipo 125 was built at Maranello by hand. In 1990, despite new levels of automation and computerization within the walls at Maranello and Modena, Ferraris are still largely handmade cars. At Ferrari, it is the definition of a handmade car that has changed the most in those forty-odd years. The legend and spirit are not gone, they have merely grown with the times.

When speaking of building Ferraris, one must choose words carefully. The makeshift area in which Ferrari workers were fabricating parts and modifying components to construct the F40 was grandly termed a production line. Taking a step back in time, as one observer said of the factory in 1958, "This was not the General Motors assembly plant at all."

I believe this to be the first in-depth look at how Ferraris have been built. Answers to questions of when road car and race car construction were first separated or when the first "assembly line" was erected have been as difficult to uncover as have some technical specifications or early race results. As with the many other histories covering Ferrari, this book is a stride forward in learning more. New information will always be found, and I welcome any discoveries or clarifications that improve the story I have presented.

Michael Dregni
Saint Paul, Minnesota
January 1990

Introduction

Northern Italians have a saying that in the south of Italy they make pasta, in the north they make money. In Maranello, they make Ferraris. Maranello is Ferrari.

Maranello, a quiet town of some 14,000 people, rests at the feet of the rugged Apennines on the grand Emilia-Romagna plain of central Italy, fifteen kilometers south of Modena. The Emilia awakens each day cloaked in the characteristic fog of the plain, which burns away by noon to reveal a hazy sunshine. In summer, the flat horizon, broken by orchards and fields and the smokestacks of small factories, is lost in heat waves. In winter, the sky is stark, cold and overcast—and still foggy.

The houses and stores and piazzas of Maranello are modern concrete, a world removed from the ancient stone villas and red-tile roofs of Tuscany, only a mountain range to the south. The people of the Emilia are industrious and pragmatic as well, far from the vivacious Romans. This is a region of technical entrepreneurs. Rare are the giant concerns, the Fiats or Olivettis. Instead, thousands of smaller factories construct everything from ammunition to race cars in workshops ranging in size from converted garages to medium-scale industrial plants run by families or cooperatives. As Enzo Ferrari wrote in one of his memoirs, "I have seen an enormous vitality in those enterprises which emanate from the family group, later to expand as oil does in water. . . . [The people of the region are] an intelligent, willing, technically prepared workforce, traditionally capable. It is a fact that here in Emilia people have always nourished a love for technical education; in this there is a real tradition. Here one does not first build factories and then look for manpower—no, here we first form men by making available the necessary technical know-how and then we erect the factories. A factory is first and foremost made up of people, then of machinery and, lastly, of bricks and mortar."

Ferrari's presence is tangible throughout Maranello. Streets are named for the heroes: viale Alberto Ascari, via Piero Taruffi, via Gilles Villeneuve and viale Ingegnere A. Dino Ferrari. The Bar Gianni boasts the spoils of a famous war—the rear spoiler from a Ferrari Formula One car—resting above the espresso machine, signed by race driver Graham Hill and other *corridori*. A second bar off the central market square is festooned with Ferrari racing flags, decorated as a medieval knight's standard in dashing colors, gothic patterns and heraldic insignia all surrounding the 1989 Tipo 640 Formula One racer. The bartender, an eighteen-year-old boy, doesn't bat an eye as a Testarossa test car hung with a makeshift *prova* plate waits at the Largo Garibaldi stoplight before disappearing in a roar of exhaust. Down a side street, another boy in blue mechanics overalls emblazoned with the Ferrari prancing horse on the chest pedals a bicycle between the factory

foundry and the Gestione Sportiva race shop; in the bicycle's rear basket rides an Electron magnesium alloy Formula One differential casing fresh from the sand molds. Vehicles everywhere in town—swarming and buzzing Vespas, Fiat 500s, garbage trucks and the ceramic factories' forklifts—all wear Ferrari stickers; the doors to stores and bars and restaurants are plastered with more. If it moves in Maranello, it has one Ferrari sticker; if it doesn't move, it has a dozen.

The Ferrari factory lords over Maranello as if it were a feudal city-state, much as Enzo Ferrari ruled his empire with a ducal air befitting the Sforzi-Visconti. The bastions of the Ferrari works are positioned throughout the town. The Dino Ferrari mechanical and engineering school, erected by Enzo Ferrari in memory of his first-born son and run by the town, is sited just off the main thoroughfare. The Gestione Sportiva, a series of nondescript buildings housing the arcane Formula One race shop, is hidden down a dead end residential street. Alongside the race works, zoned into the adjacent village of Fiorano, is the Ferrari test track, an asphalt anomaly bordered by staid homes and farmers' fields. A Ferrari museum is being constructed not far from the race shop in town; its mirror-glass-and-steel-beam structure is futuristic and showy, reflecting an image of corporate self-promotion new to Ferrari. Other small private workshops and cottage industries across town make Ferrari components on subcontracts, but their back-street entrances are faceless, rarely graced by the prancing horse emblem.

The Ferrari factory itself lines via Abetone Inferiore only a short distance from the town's main piazza, on the old road north to Modena. This complex is a jumble of mismatched and uninspiring industrial structures bound by high cement-block walls and wire fences. The modern glass-and-steel office building peers above large manufacturing shops, surmounted by a stolid square brick smokestack bearing the famous Ferrari name in its characteristic script.

On first view, it is hard to believe that this is the home of Ferrari—so unremarkable, so uninspiring. On closer examination, the works are flush with life. The courtyard bears a flow of workers in blue or red or brown or white Ferrari overalls, running from the assembly lines to cross via Abetone when the midday meal is served at the works' *mensa* cafeteria behind Ristorante Cavallino on via Fornace. The *prova* cars issue from the side entrance on via Musso with regularity, the drivers unashamedly revving the engines down the street to loosen them up before testing. Semitrucks with car carrier trailers from Maranello Concessionaires in Great Britain, Jacques Swaters in Brussels, Belgium, and other importers throughout the world exit the gates stocked with Ferraris, following the test cars to the autostrade.

Even knowing of the history and lineage that has come forth from these gates, it is impossible to imagine the activity, the excitement or the spirit within the Ferrari works. Yet between the mundane modern factory buildings and the hodgepodge of numerous additions, the walls of the original triangular Ferrari factory of 1943 are still visible.

Chapter 1

The Factory, 1929–1959
"Impromptu Craftsmanship"

Scuderia Ferrari S.p.A. was formed on December 1, 1929, to serve as Alfa Romeo's racing arm, much as Autodelta and its reincarnation under Fiat, Alfa Corse, did later on. Enzo Ferrari had gone back to his birthplace of Modena following an "apprenticeship" of twenty years behind the wheel—both literally and figuratively—with Alfa Romeo's racing division, based at the firm's works in the Milanese

Ferrari factory, Maranello, 1972
The famous entrance to the Ferrari factory was this square archway cut through the front building of the works. Looking into the historic courtyard, one could see the yellow walls of the old race shop. Many red cars, world champion drivers and famous engineers—not to mention the day-to-day employees—have come and gone through this archway. *Hilary A. Raab, Jr.*

Scuderia Ferrari, Modena, circa 1929
The home of the Scuderia Ferrari at viale Trento e Trieste, 11, on the outskirts of Modena, during its early years of racing. Note the line-up of Scuderia race transporters, with the garage doors hidden behind. The building was painted an ocher-yellow, the color of Modena. Inside was a small but well-equipped machine shop, showroom space for Ferrari's Alfa Romeo agency and single-story car bays in the rear. Ferrari's staff numbered ten to twelve employees. *Postcard, Hilary A. Raab, Jr., Collection*

neighborhood of Portello. His return to set up shop in Modena was both a homecoming and a revolt, a chance to prove himself in the eyes of his childhood compatriots as a winning racer and as a fledgling industrialist. Later in his memoirs—*Le mie gioie terribili, "My Terrible Joys"*—Ferrari wrote that he was "ferociously attached" to the region, with a true Italian sense of place and people: "In Modena, too, where I was born and set up my own works, there is a species of psychosis for racing cars that will eventually evolve into habits and create a breed of its own. Not only my own workshops are responsible for this.... What is more, the people in this part of the country are by nature of a rebellious character—they are not easy-going folk. In short, the union of blood and brain is such that the result is a type of man who is stubborn, capable and daring—the very qualities that are needed for making racing cars." In fact, Ferrari wrote, he doubted whether he should have been able to achieve such success had he not returned to Modena.

Beginnings in Modena: "A rebellious character"
Scuderia Ferrari was headquartered in the large, ornate building at number 11 viale Trento e Trieste, a short distance from the beautiful Romanesque Duomo at the center of Modena. In the early 1920s, the city was home to some 60,000 people, and Ferrari's shop was on the

Scuderia Ferrari, Modena, circa 1935
This aerial view of the Scuderia Ferrari headquarters at viale Trento e Trieste, 11, showed the garage bays in the rear, the neighboring garden and further buildings. By the time this photograph was taken, the works had expanded beyond the original building. Note the Ferrari name on the rooftop and the Alfa Romeo agency sign in the background. *Postcard, Hilary A. Raab, Jr., Collection*

An early 1946–47 brochure for Ferrari's machine tool works before car production took over showed the factory in an aerial drawing following the rebuilding after the late World War II bombing raids. This may also be the first brochure to use the characteristic Ferrari script with the long F logo.

outskirts of town, neighboring a busy horse stable—horses were more common transportation than were automobiles in that day and age. The building was large and ornate, built in the Italian Liberty style with decorative stucco walls and iron scrollwork. Three garage doors opened onto the street beneath a grand portico and balcony, which were razed in later years. Two tall gas pumps stood guard in front of the works, topped by glass globes emblazoned with the Shell gasoline logo. Enameled-metal advertisements for Pirelli tires and an Alfa Romeo badge were bolted to the outside walls. The ground floor housed the workshops, and Enzo Ferrari, his wife, Laura, and his son, Dino, born in 1932, lived above on the first floor. A huge banner proclaiming this as the home of the Società Anonima Scuderia Ferrari was draped from the first-floor windows at the side so all Modena could see. Ferrari, the business, was started.

From this unassuming shop nearby the horse stalls galloped forth Ferrari's own *scuderia,* or "stable," of Alfa Romeo racers. The team was supervised by Ferrari and supported by his general staff of former Fiat and Alfa Romeo engineers, including Vittorio Jano and Luigi Bazzi. It ran an assortment of racers from the early 6C 1750s through the P2, Tipo B P3 and 6C 2300—and even a Duesenberg. It also ran a stable of motorcycles from 1932 to 1934, racing primarily Rudges and Nortons from England. The Alfa Romeo racers were prepared and developed at Scuderia Ferrari for both customers and the team itself.

In 1934–35, the racing team became a car constructor—crossing a fine line between the race modification of factory cars and the construction of unique automobiles. Headed by Bazzi, the team designed and assembled the two twin-engined Alfa Romeo–Scuderia Ferrari Bimotore cars in less than four months. Based on an Alfa Romeo Tipo B P3 racer chassis, the Bimotore used two Tipo B eight-cylinder motors, one in front of the driver, the other behind. The two engines were coupled to a common gearbox and clutch—an intricate, brilliant display of engineering work from the small private shop inspired to combat the powerful, well-funded German factory teams.

Through the years, the history of the *scruderia* was one of victories across Italy and Europe, until the emergence of the German rivals, Mercedes-Benz and Auto Union. In 1938, Alfa Romeo took over Scuderia Ferrari with Ferrari's probably reluctant approval and ran the team directly from Milan, under the banner Alfa Corse. Ferrari served as manager.

Alfa Corse designers were constructing the famous Tipo 158 Alfetta single-seater at Portello, but much of the development work and many of the eventual modifications to make it a race winner came from Ferrari's team. Dividing his work between Modena and Milan, Ferrari initially built four Alfettas with the help of Alfa Romeo engineer Gioacchino Colombo. Ironically, the success of the Alfettas later haunted Ferrari's own efforts—all part of the incestuous family tree that made up the Italian racing world.

Ferrari was a Modenese of rebellious character, as he had stated, and soon became involved in legendary conflicts with the Alfa Romeo chief engineer, Spaniard Wilfredo Ricart. Within one year, Ferrari found being an employee intolerable. In 1939, he returned once again to Modena to spark another company, Auto Avio Costruzioni, producing machine tools and oil-driven grinding machines. Working again on viale Trento e Trieste, the shop now had a total of forty employees.

Ferrari factory, Maranello, 1952
The early engine and suspension components were machined in this long
workroom off the car assembly shops. On the tool at center, a crankshaft was
being drilled for oil passages. Behind the drill to the right, an engine block was
being machined. On the shelves to the far left rested the finished products:
crankshafts, cylinder heads and casing covers—all machined and finished
within the same shop. The machining tools were of Italian origin, of course;
Enzo Ferrari would have it no other way. *Road & Track*

Ferrari factory, Maranello, 1952
Punching out on the time clock at the end of the day. The time clock was
situated under the square archway entering the factory courtyard at the front
gates from via Abetone Inferiore. As of 1989, a time clock at the same location
was still used by Ferrari workers punching in and out in the morning, at noon
and in the evening. This time clock may have served all the factory's workers
in 1952, but in 1989, several time clocks sited in different parts of the works
were needed. Many of the new time clocks were automated, and workers used
their plastic Ferrari employee identification cards to check in and out. *Road &
Track*

Late in 1939, Ferrari was approached by two young former Scuderia Ferrari clients, Alberto Ascari and the Marchese Machiavelli, who asked him to build two cars to contest the 1940 Mille Miglia. The idea piqued Ferrari's interest. Despite an agreement with Alfa Romeo to not place his name on the hood of a race car for four years following their severance, Ferrari decided on Christmas Eve 1939 to once again begin fabricating racing cars.

Tipo 815: Ferrari, *preparatore*

The Auto Avio Costruzioni Tipo 815 cars were designed, constructed and tested at the workshop within four months by Ferrari and his team, including designer Alberto Massimino, Luigi Bazzi and test

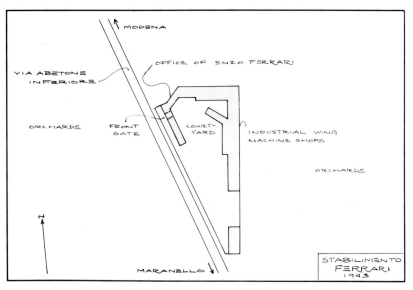

Layout of the first Ferrari factory at Maranello, 1943.

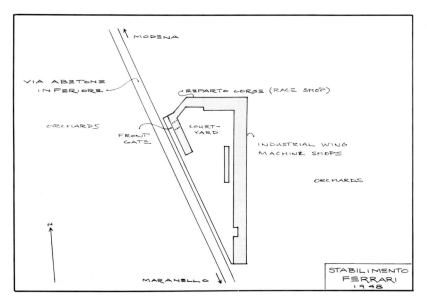

Layout of the Ferrari factory, 1948, following the rebuilding after the World War II bombardments.

driver Enrico Nardi. Like the earlier Bimotore, the Tipo 815 was an assembled car using proprietary parts but with uniquely engineered modifications and developments. Still, the car was based on a production automobile—the ubiquitous Fiat 508C 1100 cc four-cylinder Balilla.

There were several reasons for basing the Tipo 815 on a Fiat. First, parts were readily available and knowledge of tuning the cars was widespread. Second, according to Ferrari, Fiat offered cash prizes to Mille Miglia class winners using its products. Thus, Ferrari flirted with the Fiat as a *preparatore,* a "tuner" of production cars in the later style of Carlo Abarth and company. The Tipo 815 was more than just a developed Balilla, however.

Unlike the Bimotore's twin Alfa Romeo engines, the Tipo 815's inline 1496 cc eight-cylinder engine was largely original, designed and built by Ferrari's team. For a fledgling constructor, the most difficult part of the engine was fabricating the cylinder heads. Designer Massimino's notes stated that the solution was to borrow two heads from the Fiat engines. Still, the engine was not based on a simple mating of two Fiat engine blocks, but used a uniquely cast block. Ferrari did not have a foundry in the viale Trento e Trieste shop, so the castings were done on hire by Alessandro Calzoni's foundry in Bologna. The steel crankshaft was built in-house using the firm's primary product, the machine tools. Many of the other components, including the connecting rods, valves, rocker arms, crankshaft bearings and so on, were from Fiat. The two cars used Marelli distributors and Weber carburetors, which quickly became long-running staple components of Ferrari automobiles.

The Tipo 815 cars ran the 1940 Mille Miglia and showed promise before retiring with mechanical failures. This was the last Mille Miglia before World War II. With the war, automobile construction was also halted, and the Tipo 815 cars were never developed. Auto Avio Costruzioni was called upon to build war materials and grinding machines for Mussolini's conflict.

In 1943, Ferrari moved his factory away from the faithful viale Trento e Trieste building to a new facility in Maranello, but the workshop remained part of the Ferrari firm. After car construction began in Maranello, the old Modena shop served for many years as the company's offices, customer service division and delivery space for new cars.

In the 1970s, the grand old workshop was torn down and a new Ferrari customer shop was built. The new building was of red brick, fronting onto viale Trento e Trieste with a large sliding garage door that was the main entrance for cars and people, crowned by the Ferrari name in glowing yellow letters. Prominent Italian journalist and long-time Ferrari confidant Gino Rancati recalled the viale Trento e Trieste customer shop in his remembrance *Ferrari, l'unico, "Ferrari: A Memory."* "It was a long, low building . . . containing small, modest offices with mass-produced furniture and with photographs of races and racing-drivers on the walls. It was in these rooms that customers and drivers waited to see the Commendatore. His office was fairly big. There were numerous photographs reminding him of his great adventures and on a shelf next to his desk were portraits of dead drivers, and a great quantity of cups and trophies. Around the courtyard were workshops and a storage room—which was modest and badly lit—for cars that were to be dispatched to the wealthy people who had ordered them."

In the 1980s, Ferrari's second works in Modena was demolished to make room for a monstrous parking garage. Today, viale Trento e Trieste is a typical nondescript modern Modenese thoroughfare, crowded with traffic, office buildings and small grocery shops on the edge of the *centro storico,* the "historic center" of the city. A brass plaque faces drivers as they enter the well-used ramp, commemorating the site's automobile heritage.

A modern factory at Maranello

Enzo Ferrari moved his works to Maranello in response to a wartime decree from fascist dictator Benito Mussolini that ordered decentralization of Italian industry so as to not provide concentrated targets for Allied bombers. Maranello was Ferrari's second choice for the new factory site, according to Italian journalist Gianni Rogliatti. Ferrari originally looked at land in the nearby village of Formigine, but the owner decided not to sell. As Ferrari owned a house and a cherry orchard on the outskirts of Maranello, he began a search for suitable

Ferrari factory, Maranello, 1952
The beginning of the assembly process for an early road car. Ladder-frame chassis were trucked in from suppliers such as Gilco in Milan and then set up on stands to begin assembly work. The frame in the foreground was mounted upside-down for ease of labor, and the worker was routing brake lines, drilling holes in the tubing with the electric hand drill as he went. The frame in the background was rightside-up and in a more complete state, although still minus the firewall. The stands had no swivels for turning frames over; either human muscle was called upon or an overhead hoist was available. Note the proximity of the drill press at left to the actual assembly area; components could be easily modified or even fabricated there and then. A welded-up gas tank waited alongside the drill press. *Road & Track*

space there. Following negotiations with the local miller, Ferrari purchased the man's home and some land along the road to Abetone. The land became the site of the factory and the home's location later became the site of Ristorante Cavallino.

Construction of the factory began in 1943, with long, low workshops set in a triangular shape around a central tree-lined courtyard. A square arch was built through the front building to provide an entrance from the road into the courtyard. The walls of the workshops were painted a dusty ocher-yellow, the color of Ferrari's hometown of Modena just as the Ferrari insignia was later backed by a field of yellow. During the war, the company employed some 100 workers, and the building of machine tools continued. At the time, this was the only such factory in Maranello and the structures stood out against the surrounding fields and forests. Enzo Ferrari described Maranello as "an unknown village" of some 600 people, and he remembered the roads around the factory as dusty thoroughfares traversed by slow bullock carts. Those roads were soon to be ruled by red racing cars.

Where the small manufacturer of machine tools got the money to build a grand factory during the war years is a question that has never been answered. According to one story, Ferrari's wife, Laura, had money that was invested into the new works, giving her a say at least behind the scenes. Certainly, Auto Avio Costruzioni had been a success

Suppliers and Sponsors: A Society of Sub-Contractors

As a good racer should, Enzo Ferrari always thanked his suppliers and paid homage to his sponsors. Ferrari made a high proportion of his car components within the factory walls in his quest for quality and a controlling hand over engineering designs. Nevertheless, basic components such as ball bearings, fasteners, pistons, valves and the like were too specialized and time-consuming for a factory such as Maranello to fabricate, and were purchased from outside suppliers. Ferrari preferred to concentrate on building the racing cars themselves.

Only in later years did the Ferrari works racers wear decals beyond that of the prancing horse; in the early days, Ferrari's recognition of his suppliers and sponsors came in other forms. The prewar Scuderia Ferrari race transports were painted with the logos of Pirelli and Alfa Romeo, and the headquarters in Modena bore their advertising signs as well. Beginning at Maranello, mechanics and factory workers sported light blue coveralls with the Shell emblem sewn over the heart; it wasn't until later that the Ferrari insignia took Shell's place. And finally, the factory's annuals always included a thanks to the list of suppliers and sponsors.

Many of these suppliers have become famous, either in their own right or in Ferrari's shared limelight. The 1949 Annual provides insight into Ferrari's suppliers of the time.

To begin with, Ferrari gave thanks to Carrozzeria Touring of Milan for its early coachwork on the Tipo 166 *barchette*. Touring's stirring advertising copy read, "The weight is the nemesis, the wind is the obstacle. Internal metal construction. Models profiled by the wind."

C. A. "Tony" Vandervell's crankshaft main bearings were revolutionary in their thin-wall construction, overcoming fundamental problems in early Ferrari engine designs and contributing to the strength and reliability of the engines. Vandervell bearings were designed by the American Clevite company and built in England—one of the few parts from non-Italian suppliers.

Several Italian companies supplied other engine components. RIV ball bearings were long used in both Ferrari engines and Ferrari wheel hubs; the company's ad copy read, "On the road to success, the uncontested dominator." Officine Sant'Ambrogio based in Turin supplied engine valves under the trade name Livia. Timing chains came from Regina. Engine gaskets were made by Spesso & Caglieris of Turin.

Mondial pistons from Turin were the best available in Italy and were used by Ferrari for years, as well as by other racing car and motorcycle manufacturers such as FB Mondial, Parilla, Guzzi and more. The company's patriotic copy proclaimed, "Italian cars, Italian drivers, Italian products—They win and they convince."

Carburetion for almost every Ferrari from the Tipo 815 until the dawn of fuel injection came from Weber of Bologna. Edoardo Weber constructed downdraft and sidedraft carburetors specifically for Ferraris. As the ad said, Webers were "carburetors for victory, carburetors for economy."

For the Tipo 815 cars, Ferrari created a one-off wiring harness. Since then, most of the electrical equipment for Ferraris has come from Magneti Marelli, based in Milan. Marelli supplied spark plugs, batteries, race magnetos, coils, distributors, dynamo generators and small electric motors. Champion spark plugs were also used.

In the beginning, chassis were built by Gilco, the corporate name of Milan's Gilberto Colombo. Later, they were constructed by Vaccari on the northwest side of Modena.

Houdaille lever-action shock absorbers were used before the advent of the piston shock. Houdaille shocks were made by the French.

Suspension springs came from Angelo Cagnola, based in Lissone, outside Milan. Leaf front springs and semi-elliptic rear springs were purchased from A. Rejna of Milan, which also made coil springs.

Fren-do of Turin supplied brake linings and clutch surfaces.

For tires, Ferrari jumped from supplier to supplier depending on the prevailing technology in a constantly changing infant industry. Engelbert was one of the earliest suppliers; Pirelli of Turin was one of the most constant suppliers.

While the source for tires fluctuated, Ferrari stood behind the wire wheels and stamped steel wheels of Carlo Borrani of Milan. Later, Campagnolo and Cromadora alloy wheels were favored.

Fasteners—from nuts, bolts and washers to specialty circlips, studs and internal-wrenching engine bolts—came largely from OEB, or Officine Egidio Brugola, based in Lissone, outside Milan. Ferrari also fabricated some of its own specialty fasteners over the years for race cars.

As with tire manufacturers, Ferrari sided with several oil and gasoline makers through the years. In the beginning, Shell globes surmounted the gasoline pumps before the Modenese home of Scuderia Ferrari. The 1949 Annual praised Esso as being "in the service of the country." By the 1950s, Ferrari was back with Shell, as shown by the patch on the workers' coveralls and the modern Shell gasoline pumps in the courtyard at Maranello. In the 1990s, Agip's Supercortemaggiore insignia was on the cars and the gas pumps at the factory.

and some capital was available, although how much is not known. It is also possible that Ferrari's efforts were supported by the government; he was, after all, following the decree to decentralize industry and building vital wartime materials. Still, owing to the secrecy and politics of the era and the men involved, this is a point in Ferrari history that may remain untold. Historian Hans Tanner reported that Enzo Ferrari would simply not discuss the war, an era "of tremendous grief and bad memories." When asked, even Luigi Chinetti, Sr., could only shrug his shoulders.

The factory was bombarded on November 4, 1944, and again in February 1945. The last attack, late in the war, was a strategic attempt to hasten the retreat of the Germans following Italy's surrender. The destruction to the factory was immense. Many of the original brick-

Ferrari factory, Maranello, 1952
Machining the famous large racing drum brakes, nicknamed *padellone,* or big frying pans. The drums started life as an aluminum alloy casting and were laboriously machined to their finished state. Note the spray of metal shavings and the worker's lack of eye protection—or any protection at all, for that matter. *Road & Track*

Livia valves produced by Officine Sant'Ambrogio in Turin were favored by Ferrari in his early V-12 engines, as this advertisement from the 1953 Ferrari Annual stated.

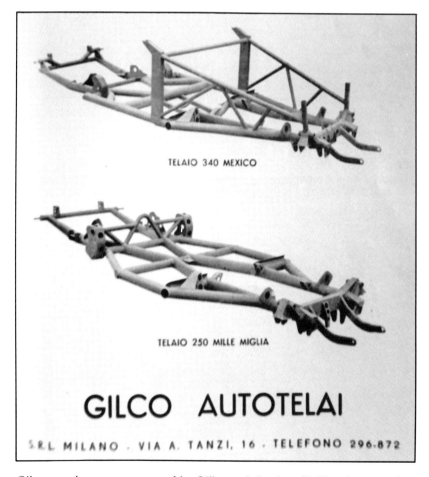

Gilco was the company owned by Gilberto Colombo of Milan that served as Ferrari's main frame builder through the 1950s. This advertisement from the 1953 Ferrari Annual showed the frames for the 340 Mexico and 250 MM.

and-timber shops were leveled, and production was slowed until the workshops could be rebuilt fully in 1946.

With the end of the war in 1945, the market for machine tools grew as Italian industry began to reconstruct itself. Throughout the war, however, Ferrari wrote that he had continued to work on racing car designs, and with the end of the wartime manufacturing regulations, his desire to build cars could be realized. Ferrari Automobili was born.

Ferrari must have played the game of politics well during the war years to emerge with his factory and reputation intact. During the era of the fascists, the Scuderia Ferrari magazine featured Il Duce on the cover, and Mussolini must have believed that Ferrari was racing for the greater glory of the party. But the team was still cheered for by the populace, who perhaps cared more for racing than for politics—and Enzo Ferrari was racing for the sake of racing.

In the political war that followed the world war in Italy, Ferrari was also a survivor. Sergio Scaglietti, who later founded Carrozzeria Scaglietti in Modena, fought as a communist partisan based in the Apennines. After the hostilities, Scaglietti joined forces with Ferrari. In an interview with an Italian publisher, Scaglietti remembered the war years and Ferrari's role: "Ferrari was anti-*Fascista*—maybe anti-*communismo,* too—but always for *l'Italia,* maybe Emilia and *numero uno,* for Ferrari! I tell you, seriously, the people were for him. He would not have trouble after the war."

With Italy in ruins following the devastation of World War II, the will and strength and foresight of Ferrari to build V–12 engined racing cars must have bordered on the extravagant, if not eccentric. The obstacles aligned against him were all but insurmountable: finding raw iron, steel, aluminum and rubber materials for car construction with the Italian industrial base still in shambles; financing the factory in an inflated and devastated economy—and who was to buy these cars and support the factory in the long term? Most of the Italian manufacturers that rebuilt empires after the war concentrated on inexpensive and economic vehicles to mobilize the country in a new way: Fiat built its Topolino; Piaggio and Innocenti designed their Vespa and Lambretta scooters; and newcomers to the market, such as Moto Ducati with its Cucciolo motorized bicycles and Iso with its Isomoto scooters and Isetta cars, developed along the same lines. Ferrari went with his passion.

By 1946, racing of both automobiles and motorcycles had resumed with fervor throughout Italy. Racers simply returned to their garages or workshops and dusted off the old cars and motorcycles left over

Ferrari race shop, Maranello, 1956–57
Race shop workers assembled a 290 MM sports racer. From 1946 to 1957, Ferrari construction techniques were much the same in the race shop and in the wing of the building where the road cars were built; in 1958, the factory erected its first assembly line for road cars, leading to a revolution in the way Ferraris were built. In the years before the line, the road car assembly was far from Henry Ford's ideal. Chassis and bodies were received from the *carrozzeria* and set atop tubework jigs to begin construction. Workers assembled components onto each car, crouching down on their knees to get at the undercarriage or bending over the body to work from the top. Here, the assemblers stood on wooden sawhorses to reach the innards; sore backs at the end of the day must have been common. *Jesse Alexander*

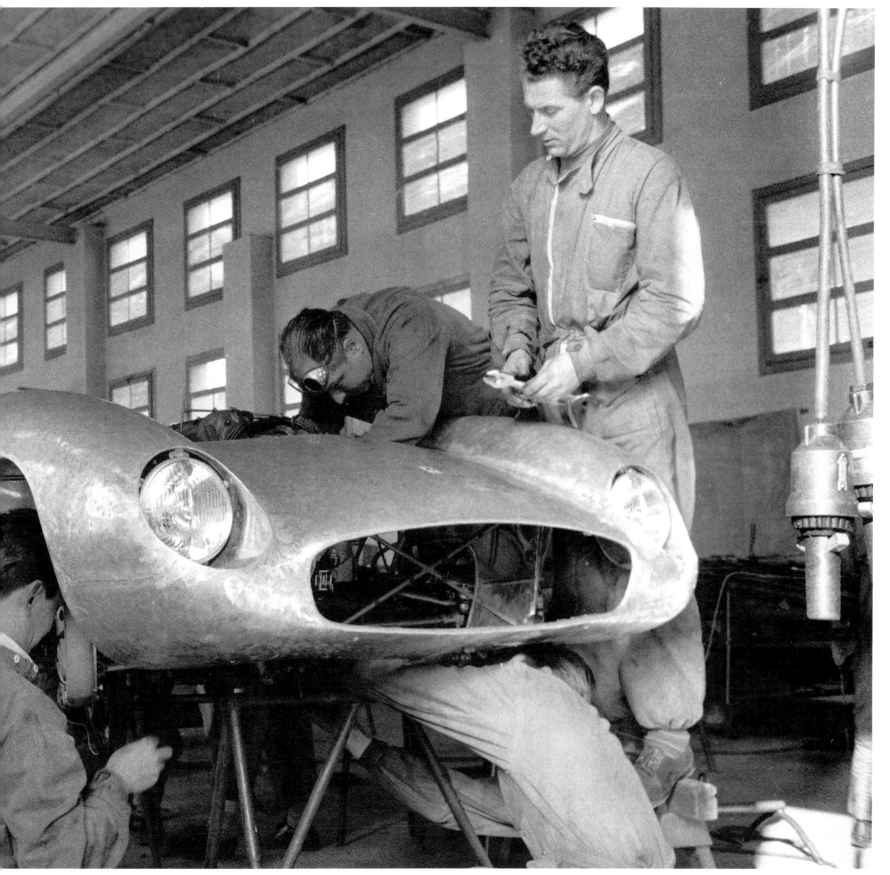

from prewar glories. Even the factories returned with their former racers: Maserati pushed out its 4 CLT and started it up; Alfa Romeo refurbished its famous Tipo 158 Alfetta; Moto Guzzi came back astride its Condor and Albatross. New racing cars and motorcycles were not constructed by the old guard for several years. Other entrepreneurs set up shop as the famed Italian *preparatori*, tuning and modifying production cars for racing. Their ranks included former Auto Avio Costruzioni Tipo 815 test driver Enrico Nardi, Carlo Abarth and Virgilio Conrero. On the motorcycle front, only Moto Parilla started up as a brand-new company and built a novel 250 cc racer immediately following the war. Ferrari was alone in his willingness to gamble all on starting a new company to develop racing cars. And he was going to take on a V–12 engine.

Even with Ferrari's heart set on racing, the mainstay production of machine tools continued at Ferrari Automobili. As the road cars would one day aid financing of the racers, sales of machine tools did the same early on. In his memoirs, Ferrari stated that once the war was finished and he could return to racing cars, he "hastily" dropped the manufacturing of machine tools. Yet it seems that the machine tools production continued for several years; accounts vary as to when this production actually ended. One long-time Ferrari machine tools salesman, as well as racing driver, was Franco Cortese. Interviewed by journalist Gianni Rogliatti, he remembered how he arrived back at the factory one day toward the end of 1945 with his book full of orders only to be told by Enzo Ferrari that he should sell no more tools; machine tools construction was at an end. In an interview with Italian writer Angelo Tito Anselmi in *Ferrari Tipo 166,* Carlo Felice Bianchi Anderloni, the director of Carrozzeria Touring, recalled that while Ferrari

was building his first automobile at Maranello in 1946–47, the Tipo 125, construction was split between cars and machine tools. Anderloni explained that "Enzo Ferrari had purely sporting ambitions and was not yet aware of the commercial and worldwide success which his cars would enjoy in a very short time. This seems to be confirmed by the fact that quite some time elapsed before he completely abandoned the production of machine tools in Maranello and devoted himself totally to the production of cars."

Work on the Tipo 125 began in 1946 with a team headed by Gioacchino Colombo and Luigi Bazzi. This time, the car was to be an original and based around an engine that was all Ferrari, unlike the Alfa Bimotore and the Tipo 815. At the end of 1946, Enzo Ferrari

PISTONE BORGO

Ferrari factory, Maranello, 1952
Tolerances on cylinder liners and a crankshaft were checked by hand with a dial micrometer. Up into the 1990s, Ferrari technical inspectors still tested tolerances on engine parts by hand. *Road & Track*

Borgo pistons were famous in high-performance Italian cars and motorcycles. This advertisement from the 1953 Ferrari Annual emphasized the horsepower possible.

called the first of his famous press conferences to introduce his new racing car, and in 1947, three Tipo 125 cars were built.

Ferrari's first success, the Tipo 166

With the Tipo 125 and the subsequent Tipo 159 of 1947, Ferrari was on the road to becoming a specialized race car constructor. From this starting point, he would move on to building Formula One cars in 1948 with the Tipo 125GP. These early cars were important in gaining early acceptance and, indeed, respect within the racing world.

In 1948, Gioacchino Colombo arrived at Maranello to stay, marking a dedication and commitment on Ferrari's part that was to rule Ferrari Automobili. In his memoirs, *Le origine del mito, "Origins of the Ferrari Legend,"* Colombo wrote that by this time Ferrari was devoted to building racing cars: "On my arrival in Maranello, Ferrari's program was completely dedicated to the building of cars. . . . Ferrari's policy was to build winning cars and sell them. As he didn't have a large industrial backing and couldn't base the costs of his sports car manufacture on large-scale commercial production, he was forced to make the racing vehicles the mainstay of his firm's work." This was Enzo Ferrari's succinct philosophy and it remained in effect for the first ten years of Ferrari Automobili.

The Tipo 166 was Ferrari's first success. From its premier outing in 1947, it was victorious in races across Europe. Its recognition came early in 1948, however, when Clemente Biondetti and Giuseppe Navone won the 1948 Mille Miglia in a 166 Sport, and Luigi Chinetti and Lord Peter Selsdon swept the 1948 Paris twelve-hour race in a 166 in September. At the first postwar running of the twenty-four-hour race at Le Mans in 1949, Chinetti and Selsdon again scored a victory in a 166 MM *barchetta.* Chinetti then won the twenty-four-hour race at Spa in Belgium with the same car. It's hard to imagine the thrill that the triumphs of the *barchette,* loosely translated as "little boats" because of their shape, must have inspired at the infant Maranello factory; certainly Ferrari had tasted victory before, but now it was all of his own doing, with cars bearing his name alone on the hood.

With the viability of the Tipo 166 proven on the international scene, the desire and demand for the cars climbed dramatically among racers. Winning races was selling cars on both the road and the track, as Colombo remembered in his memoirs. From 1947 to 1948, until Chinetti's two milestone victories, Ferrari had built a mere nine or ten Tipo 166 cars in 166 Spyder Corsa, 166 MM and 166 Sport form; following the victories and continuing well into 1953, Ferrari built a total of ninety-two Tipo 166 automobiles.

Early in the life of the 166, Ferrari also began to receive requests from nonracing customers for a road-going version. At the first auto show in which Ferrari participated, the Turin Salon of November 1948, the company unveiled its first customer road car, the 166 Inter, and the first Ferraris were sold to private parties in the same year. This increase in demand and subsequent production for the fledgling Ferrari Automobili was dramatic. The company, which had started car construction two years earlier building an average of three specialty handcrafted racers per year, was now forced into actual automobile production.

American driver Phil Hill, who would go on to win the world Formula One driver's championship and three Le Mans races for Ferrari, first visited Modena and Maranello in 1952. Hill recounted his impressions of how automobiles were constructed at Ferrari in this era of growth for the company. Ferrari's production had continued to blossom following the success of the Tipo 166, and the company was building a spectacular range of models for both the street and the racetrack—albeit in a handful of examples. Alongside the last of the 166 cars, Ferrari was making the Tipo 212 Export and Inter models, the 225 S, the 340 America and the first of its Grand Prix challengers.

Hill's first visit to Maranello came at a historic time for the factory. From the facility's founding in 1946 to 1951, all Ferrari cars were built in the same workshop. But in 1951–52, a revolution struck Ferrari car construction: production of the road cars and race cars was separated within the workshops. In just five years, Ferrari had developed to the point where a race shop was set up apart from the road car assembly shop owing to the increase in volume and specialized work required in the fabrication of both types of Ferraris. This separation also signified a changing working technique within the factory between the race car shop and the customer road car shop.

Phil Hill described the road car production line: "In terms of an assembly line, you can call it what you will, but there wasn't an assembly line in the classical sense. There was a line of cars that were going through the process with people working on them. The cars were set up on jigs and the workers pushed them along on the jigs' wheels every so often." This was far from the Henry Ford ideal and, to American eyes, much closer to the process of a specialty race shop building racing one-offs, as Hill remembered.

But what struck Hill above all was the spirit at the works. Here was a factory struggling against all odds to produce the world's foremost state-of-the-art race and *granturismo* automobiles, a David waging war with the Goliath of economics and the large-scale auto manufacturers. The factory was full of charm and romance to the young driver's eyes, the stuff of legend even then. Hill: "The factory was a long way from what it is now: the social and political changes in Italy over the past forty years have been enormous. At that time there was a broader space between workers and employers, and employees were not allowed by law to strike, as they are now. It was more than just Enzo Ferrari's iron hand. The workers and mechanics—even in the race shop—had a much more humble air, a subservient attitude, yet there was still a deep interest in what they were doing."

Supply and demand, and increased production

One of Ferrari's greatest engineers, Gioacchino Colombo, was struck by the new factory when he first arrived at Maranello following World War II. He remembered that initial reaction in his memoirs: "It was a modern factory, already quite extensive in size and now totally rebuilt in the part which had been damaged by the bombardments. The workforce was highly specialized, well-trained and equipped, with machine tools of top quality. It was a very different set-up from what one might have expected when one remembered the air of impromptu craftsmanship which had surrounded the planning phase of the first Ferrari cars. This efficient structure was in fact to be one of the key factors in the rapid success of Ferrari." Colombo's prediction would prove to be correct.

A Visit to Nardi & c., 1958

American Mark Wallach visited Enrico Nardi's steering wheel manufacturing works in Turin in 1958. Wallach was team manager for Ed Hugus' Le Mans team, and ran an automobile shop in Paris.

Nardi & c. was situated at the other end of via Vincenzo Lancia from the Lancia factory, where Nardi had worked after leaving Ferrari's Auto Avio Costruzioni and the Tipo 815. The Lancia factory was a vast array of towering smokestacks and manufacturing buildings housing a multitude of long assembly lines producing thousands of cars per year; Nardi & c. was a miniscule jumble of garages and workshops.

Nardi formed his company in 1950 following his time with Ferrari and Lancia, but he had already been constructing steering wheels for several years. His first steering wheels appeared on specialty Fiats and the like: it was a Nardi steering wheel that Tazio Nuvolari held aloft in a spectacular photograph of him entering the pits with his Cisitalia during the 1947 Coppa Brezzi in Turin, using his bare hand to turn the naked steering shaft. The first car to come standard with Nardi wheels was designed by Ferrari's old nemesis, Wilfredo Ricart's Spanish Pegaso, in 1952.

In 1958, Ferrari contracted Nardi to supply steering wheels for his cars, based on dimensions drawn up by Ferrari. Nardi's design was based on an aluminum three-spoke frame rimmed with mahogany or hickory. The center hub was of steel with the Ferrari prancing horse emblem in enamel. Nardi supplied Ferrari's steering wheels from 1958 to 1966—on a total of 1,317 racing and road cars, beginning with the 1958 model 250 Testa Rossa, according to Franco Varisco's history *Nardi*.

Turning off via Vincenzo Lancia through the entrance gates to Nardi & c. in 1958, Wallach found a long driveway aimed back into a tiny courtyard. Sheds lining the yard were filled with a few of Nardi's old racing and record cars—among them the Nardi Le Mans Bisiluro Twin Torpedo with its 750 cc Giannini engine—sadly neglected, covered with dust and beginning to rust, in the days when two-year-old racing cars were junk. Signor Nardi came out from a small office to greet Wallach with open arms and show him through the workshop of Nardi & c. To the back of the courtyard sat a small garage where a couple mechanics were at work on a car. Within Nardi's office stood a desk stacked with finished examples of the famous Nardi steering wheels. That was the whole works.

"Where is your factory?" Wallach asked Nardi.

With expansive, outstretched arms, Nardi replied, "All of Torino is my factory."

Nardi factory, Turin, 1958
American Mark Wallach stood inside the Nardi works during a visit. Here was the garage for assembling the Nardi cars—along with the odd Lancias and Fiats Nardi was so famous for tuning. Beyond the garage was a shed of derelict Nardi racers and project cars, and Nardi's office, occupied by a desk stacked with the renowned Nardi steering wheels. The actual steering wheel factory, according to Enrico Nardi, was all of Turin. *Mark Wallach*

Such was the manufacturing technique for several of Ferrari's component suppliers: subcontractors in turn subcontracted to people working out of their households, garages and backyard sheds. This use of black market cottage industry labor was an Italian economic tradition, producing everything from leatherwork, shoes and purses in Naples and the south to furniture and upholstery in Rome and much of the rest of Italy—and constructing Nardi steering wheels at dining room tables and workbenches throughout Turin. By subcontracting to cottage workers, a manufacturer could hide the extent of his or her operation from the government and the tax collector. This industrial black market has kept much of Italy's wealth hidden from economic forecasters and tallies of the gross national product since the turn of the century.

An examination of the number of automobiles produced in the years 1947–56 also sheds light on Ferrari's mode of car construction. Ferrari's first cars were one-offs: the Tipi 125, 159 and early 166. With the success of the 166, Ferrari began to build in small series, often of around a dozen cars—sometimes more, often less—until demand was satisfied or until the factory made substantial changes to the cars, initiating a new series. The cars were classified by the factory according to single-cylinder engine displacement—166, 212, 250, 340 cc and so on—but modifications were made within series to the engine as well as to the bodywork and drivetrain. In the end, each of the approximately 750 cars built in Ferrari's first ten years was a unique automobile, a

special built on a case-by-case basis, by hand and without the uniformity of a production line. When a component was needed, it was often fabricated there and then at a worktable or lathe. Much of this was made possible by the inexpensive labor of postwar Italy and the abundance of human resources.

The drive to construct all the parts possible within the factory walls reflected Enzo Ferrari's demand for maximum control over the quality of all components at all times. In 1954, a foundry was erected at the factory to cast engine casings from aluminum and magnesium alloys. Ferrari also ran a plating and heat-treating plant for chroming parts. Still, the factory did not have the tooling, expertise or finances to fabricate many parts; it was simply less expensive and easier to buy many components. Automobile makers around the world subcontract for items, and even though he wanted his cars to wear no nameplate but his own, Ferrari was no different. Thus, Ferrari has always been an assembler of cars.

Of course, outside suppliers were forced to meet Enzo Ferrari's stringent quality controls, and over the years, many of their names have justly become famous in connection with his automobiles: Marelli ignition, Borrani wheels, Nardi and Momo steering wheels, Weber carburetors, Vandervell thin-wall bearings. Electrical equipment and small motors, many engine components, tires, glass, upholstery fabrics, gauges and so on also came from suppliers.

In the years 1947 to 1956, Ferrari production at Maranello totaled 389 automobiles. From the beginnings in 1947 when the workshops built three cars, the factory made its largest leap in construction during 1949, when twenty-one cars were fabricated, an eighty-six percent increase over the first year. Through the early 1950s, the number of automobiles built each year continued to climb until in 1953 Ferrari constructed fifty-seven cars, just over one per week. Production must have been running near capacity for the small workshops, as in the next two years only a handful more cars were built—fifty-eight in 1954 and sixty-one in 1955.

While the construction of automobiles climbed steadily from 1947 to 1956, the physical size of the factory extended much more slowly. The original Maranello works was rebuilt in 1946 following the Allied bombardments, but the shops went relatively unchanged in terms of floor space. In 1948, the first addition was made to the original triangular structure, adding only a quarter again more space at best. It was fourteen years until the next addition was made to the factory, in 1962.

The number of employees grew more quickly, meeting the increase in car construction, but remained well below the percentage increase in number of automobiles finished. Car construction escalated ninety-six percent from 1947 to 1956; over the same period, the numbers of workers climbed only forty-four percent. Ferrari set up shop in Maranello in 1943 with some 100 workers. The ranks increased to 140 in 1946 when automobile production began. By 1955, that number had not even doubled, to 250 workers.

The parking garage that had taken over the city block in Modena where the first home of Scuderia Ferrari and the later Ferrari Assistenza were located. The small plaques mounted on the concrete pillar note the history of the site.

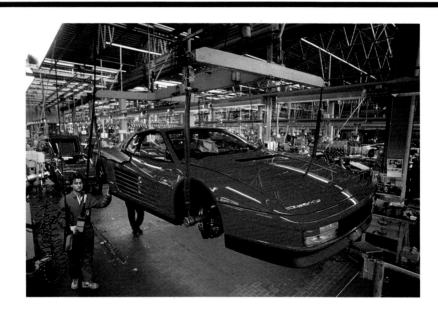

Chapter 2
The Factory, 1960–1990
The Production Lines Roll

In 1954, Ferrari introduced the forerunner to its most successful car series ever, the 250 GT. The first 250 GT long-wheelbase, serial number 0357 GT, was based on the earlier 250 MM and 250 Europa, a Mille Miglia racer and a *granturismo berlinetta*. Over its ten-year life span, the 250 GT series was refined through several guises—from *berlinetta* to long-wheelbase Tour de France through to short-wheelbase, lightweight Comp. 61 cars, luxurious Spyder California and GTO. The car won converts on the road and trophies on the tracks.

Ferrari factory, Maranello, 1959
Ferrari's first assembly line in full swing, constructing several 250 GT Pinin Farina Coupes and a sole early 250 GT Scaglietti Berlinetta. This single press release photograph detailed almost the complete Ferrari road car production shop. Beginning at bottom left, the chassis were set up on jigs to be built onto; the chassis were subcontracted out and had been trucked to the factory. Moving up this line of chassis, the suspension, steering and other driveline components were added, until the end of the line when the bodywork was lowered onto the chassis. All nice and neat. But then, the car had to return to the parallel assembly line, which started all the way back at the other side of the shop. Given the space, the cars must have been carried on the overhead hoist to the start of the assembly line. *Ferrari S.p.A., Peter Coltrin Collection, courtesy Hilary A. Raab, Jr.*

Beyond the fame it brought to Ferrari's name, the 250 GT series also introduced revolutionary changes to Ferrari Automobili.

250 GT series
The 1960s were the glory years of Ferrari. Maranello was racing more cars than ever before at numerous levels and winning in all. Spirits at the factory were high and enthusiasm was everywhere in the years before the constant labor strikes and discontent of the 1970s. And Ferrari had a road car in the 250 GT series that was performing as never before in terms of mechanical quality, customer sales and factory revenue.

Whereas the Tipo 166 was Ferrari's first success, the 250 GT series was perhaps the factory's greatest accomplishment. During the ten years of the 250 GT series, the Maranello factory more than doubled in physical size and started rolling with its first true assembly

Ferrari factory, Maranello, 1989
Off to one side of the modern twin assembly lines, a shorter, smaller line constructed Testarossas. Painted and trimmed bodies arrived from Pininfarina with electrics and gauges attached to begin the final assembly at Maranello. Here, a worker guided a body with a mechanical hoist onto a stationary jig where the engine would be added.

Ferrari factory, Maranello, 1959
The machining sector of the factory contained rows of machine tools and lathes. It also had ample work space and natural light—this was the "modern factory" Gioacchino Colombo was so impressed by upon his arrival at Maranello. *Ferrari S.p.A., Peter Coltrin Collection, courtesy Hilary A. Raab, Jr.*

line. In the meantime, on May 23, 1960, Ferrari Automobili was re-formed as a joint stock company, SEFAC, or Società Esercizio Fabbriche Automobilistiche e Corse, S.p.A. Beyond such growth and refinements in production techniques, the way and spirit in which Ferrari automobiles were built changed forever as well.

The reasons Ferrari was able to grow so during this period were myriad. The economy of Italy was starting to flourish again following the rebuilding period after World War II, which provided a firmer foundation for Ferrari to expand upon. The economies of the other European countries had also recovered and were developing as a market for expensive sports and *granturismo* cars. The economy of America had refurbished itself earlier, but Americans were that much more removed from the renown of Ferrari's name. Still, after a slow

start for Ferrari in America, race driver Luigi Chinetti, who did so much for building Ferrari's respect in Europe with the Tipo 166, began to import Ferrari automobiles to the United States and eventually sparked his North American Racing Team. American demand for Ferraris soon outran supply.

The increased road cars sales worldwide also provided Ferrari the capital necessary for expansion. Stories have been told of the long waiting lists for Ferrari cars from the Tipo 166 on; of the demand for early racing Ferraris in America and the supply's being limited to last year's model at best; of customers arriving at the factory gates, waiting for hours to see Ferrari himself to place their order, and finally giving up and turning around to Maserati in Modena. The demand may have existed from the beginning, but it was not until 1956–62 that Ferrari

A Brave New World, circa 1955
Car Construction at Aston Martin, Mercedes-Benz, and Chevrolet

The year 1955 was a momentous one for the world's prestigious sports car makers. Aston Martin introduced the updated version of its DB2/4 as the Mk. II with mechanical improvements and a subtly reworked body. Mercedes-Benz was capitalizing on its racing success following the debut of the 300 SL gull-winged coupe for the road. On the other side of the Atlantic, the world's first mass-production sports car with fiberglass bodywork, Chevrolet's Corvette, was available with the new small-block V-8 engine that would lead the race in the United States for years to come. And Ferrari had just introduced the first of the 250 GT series that would point out the future for Maranello. A brave new world was dawning.

Because of World War II, it had taken almost ten years for the European auto makers—most notably, Mercedes-Benz in Germany—to get back on their feet. Only Chevrolet in the United States was fully operational immediately following the war. A look inside the factories of Aston Martin, Mercedes-Benz and Chevrolet in 1955, at the construction of sports cars at least similar in goal to those of Maranello, provides some insight into Ferrari's work technique.

Aston Martin DB2/4 Mk. II
The Aston Martin works at Feltham was probably the most old-fashioned and behind-the-times after the war—and the newer works at Newport Pagnell still may have ranked so in comparison with the others in 1990. During the war, the factory had constructed aircraft components for the Supermarine Spitfire and others. Soon after the war, the company was in financial trouble and was bought by David Brown, an industrialist and tractor builder, bringing to Aston Martin a foundation of capital similar to that of Lamborghini, some ten years later.

By 1949, the works returned to Le Mans with the prototype to its DB2, a road car that led the way for Aston Martin until the debut of the DB4 in 1958.

Photographs of the updated DB2/4 Mk. II being constructed at Feltham in 1955 show one large room with cars parked haphazardly throughout, undergoing assembly. No assembly line or even line of cars atop jigs, as at Ferrari at this time, was in evidence. Workers clustered around the cars, worktables were scattered where needed with tools and equipment at hand. The lighting was dim, provided by hanging overhead lamps—nothing like the rows of windows bathing the Ferrari workshops in ample natural light.

Even into the 1960s with the construction of the DB6 at Newport Pagnell, the factory looked jammed with cars and workers—so packed together, in fact, that there was hardly room to open car doors to get inside them.

Bodywork for the DB2/4 Mk. II was formed on a so-called English wheel, a viselike handpowered tool that required finesse, time and some muscle to shape the steel and aluminum sheets. Finishing work was done with metalworking hammers and steel planishing tables. Panels were then butt-welded together and fastened to the steel frame.

Total construction of the DB2/4 Mk. II amounted to some 199 cars in a two-year period, certainly within Ferrari's realm at the time. Assembly techniques of the DB2/4 Mk. II appeared much the same as at Maranello before Ferrari's erection of the assembly line. Still, the Italian factory could boast more space, light and, possibly, better working conditions.

Mercedes-Benz 300 SL
Photographs of the 300 SL production from 1954–55 showed two assembly lines with perhaps twenty cars being built at one time. The factory was spacious, modern and spotlessly clean. Skylights in the roof and lines of fluorescent lamps provided working light. Overhead hoists allowed workers to get to the undercarriage easily and efficiently. All in all, the works was much to the stereotypical Teutonic image.

Such organization was needed considering the ambitious number of 300 SL coupes and roadsters built from 1954 to 1963–64: a total of some 4,000 cars. In 1955 alone, approximately 830 cars were constructed. In the same year, Ferrari built a total of sixty-one road cars of several models, and Chevrolet produced only 674 of the third-year Corvettes.

This large production run allowed Mercedes-Benz to make substantial investments in the construction of the car. Tooling for machine-stamping of body panels was possible, so panels could be pressed from steel in minutes—and each panel was identical, versus the hand-beaten panels on Ferraris that differed in subtle ways. The doors, hoods and trunk lids for the 300 SL were made by the several subcontracted *karosseri* from aluminum, probably with an electric power hammer, a tool Ferrari's *carrozzerie* did not use until the late 1960s.

The chassis frames for the 300 SL followed Italian engineering practice, based on the use of tube-frame chassis. As with the Ferraris, frames were fabricated atop jigs that held the tubes in place for hand-welding work.

Chevrolet Corvette
While the 300 total 1953 Corvettes were still being mostly handbuilt on makeshift lines at Chevrolet in Flint, Michigan, General Motors had big plans for the 1954 cars. Assembly lines were being erected at a new factory in St. Louis, Missouri, and tooling was prepared for high-volume production. The goal was to build and sell more than 10,000 Corvettes in 1954.

Early in 1954, Chevrolet realized that the public was not ready for its sports car; total construction for the year would finish at some 3,640 cars, with almost a third of those unsold. For 1955, management cut back its dreams and built only 674 of the 1955s. Little did Chevrolet expect that the 1955 model with its new V-8 small-block engine would point out the future success of the Corvette.

The first pilot production line had built Corvettes by hand, and each car was essentially a prototype in the best Ferrari tradition. Fiberglass panels were hand-sanded, workers used paintbrushes to apply resin and rivets were set by hand. Even in the paint booth, cars were sprayed with hand-held air guns. Three cars were finished each day.

With the production line in St. Louis in 1954–55, work was highly mechanized and automated in the tradition of archrival Henry Ford. Workers were assigned specific jobs—one man, one bolt—and the work became less personal. Cars moved along the line, stopping for a maximum of ten minutes at each work station. Fifty cars could be finished daily. Thus, in less than two years, the Corvette had gone from a handbuilt special to a production line car.

Ferrari factory, Maranello, 1958
A long-wheelbase 250 GT Spyder California chassis was constructed in the assembly shop. Photographs of the road car and race car production showed little difference in work technique—although the differences were there. In both shops, chassis were set atop jigs and built one by one. In the race shop,

however, the chassis and components would be fabricated there and then; here in the road car shop, the chassis was trucked in from a subcontractor such as Gilco in Milan or Vaccari in Modena and components were constructed in an adjacent wing of the factory. *Road & Track*

Carrozzeria Pinin Farina, Grugliasco, circa 1960
The wiring harness, relays and fuses were added to a 250 GT on the Pinin Farina line. Typically, the engine was lowered into the car at Maranello. Since the body would not have a chassis below it at this stage in construction at Pinin Farina, this "engine" was probably a silver-painted wooden mockup, used for positioning components around it; note the large wooden blocks resting atop the engine where the carburetors and air cleaner would eventually sit. Such mockups were often used in show cars as well. The battery tray provided a handy shelf for hammer and pliers, essential tools for making wiring harnesses fit into tight spaces. *Pinin Farina, courtesy Automobile Quarterly*

was able to satisfy at least some of it with higher production output and the start of a dealer network with foreign importers. Before that, a customer had to visit the factory to place his or her order for a Ferrari.

As well as providing capital to expand the factory, the commercial success of the 250 GT series also put money where Enzo Ferrari wanted it most: into the race team. As Colombo noted on his arrival, Ferrari's early philosophy was dedicated to the building of race cars, as he didn't have large industrial backing and couldn't base the manufacturing costs of his limited-edition specials on large-scale commercial production. Suddenly, here was success for Ferrari, and the factory's racing efforts in the next years were due at least in part to this influx of funding. Furthermore, the 250 GT was doing its part on the racetracks of the world; in fact, the works team and the privateers were winning more races than ever before, beginning with Alfonso de Portago's first win in a 250 GT, a Pinin Farina competition *berlinetta,* at Nassau in 1955.

Credit for the success was also due the car itself. With the 250 GT, Ferrari's first Tipo 125 car and Colombo's Tipo 125 V–12 engine had reached new heights in development. Ferrari's technique of building a car with ongoing improvements component by component based on lessons learned with the competition versions found its optimal

expression with the 250 GT series, making the cars some of the best Ferraris then or now. The Colombo Tipo 128 engine was revised with a series of minor variants, all in search of mechanical perfection: piston weights were varied, connecting rods were strengthened, ignition timing was revised, new cylinder heads were developed, and on and on. The first 250 GTs were produced much as the Tipo 166 cars some five years earlier, with each car at least partly a unique model, and not until the car was established could Ferrari see the possibilities in making the giant's step to series production on an assembly line.

The car was the work of Ferrari's team of engineers, designers and assemblers. Perhaps at no other time in the factory's history did the engineering staff include such a stellar array of talent as it did over a

Carrozzeria Pinin Farina, Grugliasco, circa 1960
On the assembly line, an array of chrome detail parts for the 250 GT—from interior window cranks to turn signal rings—were all neatly laid out and ready for assembly to the body. The workers used just screwdrivers to add the parts to the car. From photographs, the Pinin Farina works appeared much more

organized than Ferrari in terms of worktables systematized with all the components to be added to a car. At Ferrari, components had to be carried from shelves along the outside walls onto the assembly line, and then bolted to the car. *Pinin Farina, courtesy Automobile Quarterly*

ten-year period surrounding the 250 GT series: Vittorio Jano, Giotto Bizzarrini, Mauro Forghieri, Luigi Bazzi, Alberto Massimino and racing manager Romolo Tavoni.

The man who spearheaded much of Ferrari's technical drive of the 1960s was Carlo Chiti. The former Alfa Romeo engineer came to Ferrari as racing technical director in 1958, and was instrumental in developing the Formula One cars and the Le Mans prototypes. His race work perhaps stimulated much of the inspiration at Maranello, but he was himself amazed by the creative spirit and whirlwind of activity at the factory, as he told Italian writer Piero Casucci in *Chiti Grand Prix:* "The rhythm of work that Ferrari imposed on me has never left me. It made one's head spin. I don't think there has ever been another organization that could get through the same amount of work, so quickly, as the Ferrari technical office did. . . . The technical office drew up plans like an accounts office issues invoices. I've never come across handpicked staff like Ferrari had then."

Ferrari was especially proud of his team, and looked back with fond memories at the great team spirit possible in a small company such as his. The company was at a point where some of the old guard, the men of the original Scuderia Ferrari of Modena, were disembarking and fresh engineers were coming aboard. Ferrari termed the exchange of ideas "dramatic," as well as "keen and enthusiastic," and was impressed by the possibilities: "It is my opinion, in fact, that there is little which remains to be invented in automobile engineering, although there is still much room for improvement. . . . It is consequently not so much inventions which are needed as conscientious elaboration." It was this elaboration that Ferrari's staff performed so admirably with the 250 GT series.

Ferrari factory, Maranello, 1959
The exterior of the production car assembly line, looking into the center factory courtyard and north toward the race shop at the end of the alleyway. Within the workshop was a 250 GT Pinin Farina Coupe at the end of the line, awaiting wheels and tires. Note the cobblestone alley and the trees still growing in the courtyard. The Fiat truck at left was one of the race transporters. *Ferrari S.p.A., Peter Coltrin Collection, courtesy Hilary A. Raab, Jr.*

Assembly lines come to Ferrari

New Zealander Bob Wallace was at work in the Ferrari race shop when the factory's first assembly line was set up. At age twenty-one, he had journeyed from the other side of the world to be at the heart of racing. He first visited Ferrari in 1959 and worked in the race shop in 1960-61, before leaving to become Lamborghini's test and development driver for the next twelve years. Speaking in his characteristically gruff voice from his current Phoenix, Arizona, shop, Bob Wallace Cars, he remembered the revolution at Maranello: "The assembly line was set up in a rather crude manner. It was not very sophisticated, but it evolved and developed over the years as it needed to and as more money became available."

Ferrari initiated its first assembly line in 1958-59, resulting in an output of 183 automobiles, almost a doubling in production over the rate of the previous year and a dramatic increase over the rate of five years earlier when Ferrari first made just over one car a week.

The line was set up on a raised runway with the cars passing at about head-height, allowing workers to assemble cars atop the runway and to work on the undercarriage at the same time. As before, the cars were mounted on wheeled jigs that were hoisted onto the runway by an overhead crane at the start and lowered down again at the end; the luxury of ramps was not known at Ferrari for several more years.

Although the assembly line was a large step for the factory, that step had only been made halfway. Alongside the line were stationary jigs with car frames being worked on one by one, just as in the days of

the Tipo 166 or as was the practice in the race shop. Lathes, other machine tools, welding torches and gas tanks also shared the work space with the modern line, as some components were fabricated there and then while cars were being assembled. Even with the assembly line, Ferrari had hardly lost touch with its craftsman roots.

In about 1960, the overhead assembly line was expanded and lengthened to include two side-by-side runways for cars. Thus, a total of some ten cars could be assembled at one time, versus four on the single line. The dual assembly line remained in place, albeit larger and modernized, until construction of the 308 GTB series started in 1975.

The erection of assembly lines required radical new restructuring to have a good stock of components, both those built within the factory and its foundry and those arriving from outside suppliers. Whereas with the previous construction techniques components might be fabricated while constructing the car, with the larger scale of production and the desire to speed up the production rate a stock of parts was now needed. In the past, cars could wait for a component while employees worked on other features of the car; with the assembly line, the flow of materials had to be regulated and continuous. There is no record that outside suppliers were used more often by the factory at this period to make up for any deficiencies within the works, so Ferrari must have gone through a major reorganization to supply the assembly lines from the same size workshop and only a slightly larger work force.

Wallace recalled that the Ferrari assembly line was surprisingly well systematized. Parts shelves and worktables followed the line and

Ferrari, Maranello, circa 1960
This publicity photograph showed the famous front entrance to the factory, looking across via Abetone Inferiore from via Fornace. The front of the factory was little changed as of 1990, with the main entrance to the courtyard still by way of the square brick arch. *Ferrari S.p.A., Museo dell'Automobile Carlo Biscaretti di Ruffia*

Ferrari factory, Maranello, 1979
A photograph captured the mood inside the alleyways between buildings at Ferrari on a typically overcast day in Emilia. The bright white building at center was the new paint shop, along with the smokestack topped by the characteristic Ferrari script. Trees still grew within the factory walls. *Peter Coltrin, courtesy Road & Track*

were stocked with components to be added onto the car. Wallace continued: "There could be hold-ups, with parts not available and such—there always were and there always will be—but overall it was pretty well organized." Well into the 1980s, the control of components supply was a trial to Ferrari, especially with such out-of-series specials as the 900 car limited-edition run of F40s.

Later in the 250 GT series, a further change to production technique was made in accord with the assembly lines. Ferrari's previous cars and the early 250 GTs had been built at Maranello starting with the assembly of suspension components to the bare frame. The engine, radiator, transmission, front and rear axle, and wheels including the spare were then added, and in some cases the exhaust system was also bolted in place. Next, the rolling chassis was trailered, or even at times driven, to the specified coachbuilder to have a body constructed and welded in place. The body was normally painted and fitted with the complete interior, instruments, electrics and lights. It was then transported back to Ferrari for finishing and testing.

The order of car construction was now reversed. From a design by Pinin Farina, the body was made into metal by either Pinin Farina or Scaglietti. It was then transferred complete with paint, interior, instruments, electrics and lights to Maranello, where it was joined with the rolling chassis on the Ferrari assembly line. This practice continued into the 1990s, although Scaglietti's upholstery and paintwork moved to Maranello in the late 1970s.

By 1960, car completion at Maranello was at 306 per year, more than one car per working day. From the view of the 1990s, this production was merely prosaic, but when considered in connection with the factory's size and work force—and the changes in their sizes over those of earlier years—the growth was staggering.

Ferrari had yet to add on work space to the original triangular-shaped factory following the last small addition in 1948, and overall floor space was some 18,000 square meters, or 194,000 square feet. Thus, the new assembly lines were set up in the same area as the cars were formerly assembled one by one on jigs. The shop space was refigured for efficiency to double and then triple output. At the same time, the workforce numbers grew by only half. In 1955, Ferrari had a workforce of 250 people; by 1960, it employed 370. How many were directly involved in assembling cars versus office workers is not known.

In 1962, Ferrari built onto the original factory, adding some 7,000 square meters, or 75,000 square feet, of floor space and almost doubling the work space with further room for assembly. In 1965, the number of employees was increased to an estimated 500. Production continued to climb, and by the finale of the 250 GT series, the 250 GT Berlinetta Lusso of 1964, the factory was constructing 654 cars per year.

Product homogeneity: The exception was the rule

With the 250 GT series, Ferrari was still building a relatively small number of automobiles, yet in a wide array of models. From the first 250 GT, one side of the family had branched out into a competition series from the long-wheelbase Tour de France to the short-wheelbase alloy-bodied Berlinetta Comp. cars on to the 250 GTO and

Proprietary Parts: Incestuous Relationships

Ferrari has always been largely an assembler, as were many other Italian sports car manufacturers. Components such as electrical equipment, lights, wheels and tires, many basic engine subcomponents and so on were shared among Ferrari, Maserati, Lamborghini, Alfa Romeo, Fiat and the rest. Turn signals for certain 250 GT series cars were also common to Alfa Romeo models, taillights for the Lamborghini Jarama were also used on the De Tomaso Pantera and so on. All in all, the relationship between many of the Italian sports cars was incestuous in terms of proprietary parts.

Ferrari historian Dean Batchelor remembered the 1958 Boano-Ellena 250 GT coupe he purchased in 1964, which taught him many lessons concerning Ferrari's use of proprietary parts.

The car, serial number 0821 GT, had the standard 2953 cc V-12 engine with hairpin valve springs, siamese intake ports, "inside" spark plugs and a single distributor fed by two coils. Because the single distributor cap had two coil terminals and twelve spark plug terminals, the terminals were located in close proximity, tending to short out on the inside of the cap. (The cap, incidentally, was identical to the one used by Maserati on the 3500 GT, which had a twin-ignition six-cylinder engine.) A new distributor cap could not be found, but Batchelor did track down four used ones. The best of the four was selected, and the shorted area—which was visible as a line from one terminal to the next—was ground out and filled with sealing wax. The modified cap worked perfectly for many years.

The distributor rotor was also bad, and Batchelor took it with him when he went to New York in April 1966 for the annual auto show. While in New York, he went to the showroom of US Ferrari importer Luigi Chinetti. Handing Chinetti the rotor, Batchelor asked if any were in stock. Chinetti didn't bother to respond, but walked to the parts counter, handed the rotor to the parts man and walked off. The parts man disappeared for a few minutes and came back with a new rotor. The price was, as Batchelor recalled, $15.95 plus tax. But it was the right part.

In June 1966, Batchelor was in Modena visiting American expatriot photographer Pete Coltrin and told of his visit to Chinetti's. Coltrin said, "Let's go see my mechanic." The two walked a few blocks to the shop where Coltrin took his Alfa Romeo for service, and Coltrin described the rotor in Italian to the mechanic, who responded in Italian. Coltrin translated the information for Batchelor: it was a Fiat part and could be bought retail in Modena for about $3.95.

The car's heater, most of the switches, the door lock and the window crank mechanisms were Fiat parts, and were also used on several Alfa Romeo models. Italian body makers normally utilized proprietary parts as much as possible to keep the cost of a custom body within reason.

The family tree of components could also extend beyond Italy's borders. After a front end collision, American enthusiast Bert Anakin's 250 GT Lusso was left with a broken headlamp and a damaged headlamp bezel. A new bezel would have run nearly $100 if purchased from a Ferrari dealer. By chance, Anakin found that the Lusso bezel was identical to the one used on his wife's Peugeot 404 and bought a replacement for under $20.

the once-removed 250 LM. On the other side of the family was the increasingly elegant 250 GTE and 250 GT Lusso, related to the 250 Cabriolet. The Spyder California was in turn related to the 250 Tour de France and short-wheelbase Berlinetta. Within the series, bodywork by different *carrozzerie* produced essentially different cars. As Ferrari wrote in his memoirs, "The demands of mass-production are contrary to my temperament, for I am mainly interested in promoting new developments." This was an explanation; Ferrari did not bother to justify.

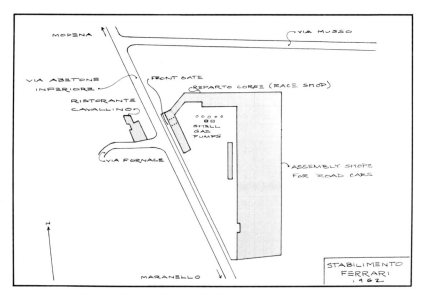

Layout of the Ferrari factory, 1962. The first major additions had been made to the works since the rebuilding in 1946, with expansion for the production car assembly area. The Ristorante Cavallino was opened on the site of the former Cavallino Bianco bar.

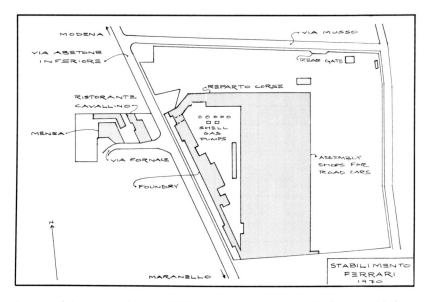

Layout of the Ferrari factory, 1970. Further expansion to the factory added on more room to the production car assembly areas. The *mensa* cafeteria was also built in this period. The factory was now fenced in.

Still, with the assembly lines, Ferrari had indeed moved forward—if not toward mass production, then toward systematizing car construction. The shelves and parts bins stocked with components to add to the cars on the lines were vital to this. Yet even with this systemization, homogeneity between cars of the same model was not assured. By the end of the 250 GT series in 1964, the Berlinetta Lussos rolling off the line were the most identical, car to car, of any Ferrari to date, but subtle detail and component source differences saved them from being clones.

The assembly lines themselves were one reason for this. Ferrari was building such small numbers that at any one time the dual lines included a wide selection of 250 GT series cars being constructed. Thus components could be shared by a 250 GT Pinin Farina Cabriolet and a 250 GT Scaglietti Berlinetta one day, and be dissimilar the next week when one batch of factory-made or subcontracted parts ran out and a new batch arrived.

Yet with Ferrari, the exception was the rule. Just when Ferrari was erecting its assembly lines for series-built automobiles, it was also constructing more special-order cars than ever before. Customer special-order cars varied either in minute extra features, such as special upholstery hides or custom instrumentation, or in one-off bodywork such as that of the 250 GT Cabriolet 1737 GT, with its 400 Superamerica-styled panels, hard top, glass sunroof and so on. These changes could be made at a *carrozzeria* or could be listed as an add-on to the factory's build order accompanying the car down the assembly line. On one hand, the Ferrari option list was nonexistent; on the other hand, it was as long as a customer's pocket was deep.

The bodywork of the 250 GT series was also officially experimented with countless times over the model's life span, and minor changes to the bodywork—from wheel arch profiles to hood scoops to vents—were continuous through the series. Ferrari used a variety of coachbuilders and by doing so searched for the ideal expression of the car. Even within one coachbuilder's styling, subtle and not-so-subtle changes were made owing to Enzo Ferrari's command or the vagaries of hand-beating body panels.

Carrozzerie yearned to be allotted a Ferrari chassis as a basis to show off the coachwork they were capable of. Nothing drew attention at an automobile show as much as a Ferrari did, making the Maranello cars the ideal vehicles to in turn display flowing new body designs or

Following page
Carrozzeria Scaglietti, Modena, 1962
The prototype 250 GTO serial number 3223 GT was fabricated in the Maranello race shop; subsequent "production" GTOs were built on an assembly line within the main production car workshop, although it's not clear whether the GTOs were built on the same assembly line as the other cars. This GTO was being constructed at Scaglietti, set atop tubular jigs. The body had been painted gray or metallic gray by the *carrozzeria*—the car was probably serial number 3851 GT, 3909 GT or 4115 GT. Here, electrics were being inserted; the Ferrari logo was probably added later at Maranello. Scaglietti did not have a true assembly line until the late sixties when the volume of work on the Dino and first 365 GTB/4 demanded the organization. Note the essential, ever-present hammer resting against the wall within easy reach. *Robert Bodin Collection*

Model Designations: Number Folklore

Beginning with the Tipo 815, Ferrari models have been designated by several systems of numbering based on the engine of the car. Only a few Ferraris have been named after famous races, such as the 365 GTB/4 Daytona and 250 Le Mans, or after the inspired bodywork, such as the 410 and 400 Superamericas and 250 GT Spyder California. And even with these cars, the engine comes first. That Ferraris are named after their engines seems only fair: the engines are what made Ferrari automobiles famous, from the Testa Rossa to the Quattrovalvole V–8. The race victories are for record books, and even the bodywork designation receives only a one-line mention at the end of a Ferrari's build sheet.

The Tipo 815 set the stage for the model designations to follow, although the system was changed when true Ferrari production began after World War II. The Tipo 815 was named for its eight-cylinder engine of 1500 cc displacement.

The first Ferraris of 1947 were designated by a numbering system based on the capacity in cubic centimeters of one cylinder of the engine. The first cars were thus designated Tipo 125 for the V–12 engine with 125 cc per cylinder for a total displacement of 1500 cc. The Tipo 159 with a larger bore and stroke, and thus larger displacement, followed.

The number designations are rounded off to the next-highest whole number: for example, a Ferrari 250 GT actually has 246.1 cc per cylinder and a 500 Mondial has 496.2 cc.

The first Dino, the 206, also gave birth to a new numbering system, combining displacement in liters and number of cylinders in a reversal of the Tipo 815 system. A 206 Dino had a 2.0 liter engine and six cylinders. The Dino series continued its designation through to the 308 GT4. The 308/208/328/348 GTB series also used this system, adding proof to the discovered prototype mockup that the original intention was to market the 308 GTB series as a Dino car.

Several exceptions to the rules cropped up. The 410 and 400 Superamericas and 500 Superfast did not follow either system. The 118 and 121 LM of the mid 1950s also did not follow the systems, although it is believed that these were internal Ferrari work codes.

In the late 1980s, Ferrari model designations for the most part followed tradition, although with an emphasis on marketing. The Testarossa revived the former 250 Testa Rossa's name, albeit in a single word, instead of being designated the 412 GT4 BB; the same held true for the Mondial V–8. The 288 GTO, on the other hand, followed the displacement-per-cylinder system. The F40 was named for Ferrari's fortieth anniversary of race car manufacturing rather than following either system or using the Ferrari work code of F120.

Carrozzeria Pinin Farina, Grugliasco, circa 1960
In 1959, Pinin Farina moved from its old shop in Turin to a modern, expanded factory in Grugliasco. The move was largely due to the increase in production at Maranello with the 250 GT series; the demands from Ferrari for bodywork had grown beyond the capabilities of Pinin Farina's former shop. The new

works was quite impressive, with a total of four assembly lines visible in this photograph. Bodies were formed in another wing, painted and partially assembled, including electrics, interiors, lighting, body detail pieces, bumpers and so on. They were then shipped to Maranello, where they were mated with the chassis. *Pinin Farina, courtesy Automobile Quarterly*

radical modernistic sculptures. The two 250 GTs bodied by Nuccio Bertone and penned by his young designer Giorgetto Giugiaro were free-lance efforts to win Ferrari's business; at the least, the cars got noticed by others. Other *carrozzerie* from Piero Drogo to Medardo Fantuzzi to the virtual unknowns such as Antonio Fontana searched out wrecked Ferrari chassis to build their reputations on. The 1960s saw the *carrozzerie* at their zenith of custom work and modifications.

Drogo had taken up aerodynamics where Giotto Bizzarrini left off, forming special bodies for 250 GTOs; Fantuzzi constructed a spyder for Chinetti's NART on a 250 GTE chassis; Zagato built several lightweight racers based on 250 GT series cars; Michelotti, Neri e Bonacini and others were also busy. Thus, Ferrari had the coachbuilders at his door and did not even have to knock at theirs.

The subcontracting of coachbuilding to the wide selection of

Ferrari factory, Maranello, 1972
The raised two-runway assembly lines were in full swing here. The line at left was given over to building solely 246 GT and GTS Dinos, while the line at right constructed a mix of V–12 engined 365 GTB/4 and 365 GTC/4 cars. A single assembly line was first erected in 1958 to produce 250 GTs. In about 1960, the second runway was added. These twin lines remained in operation with little change until the 1980s, when production of the 308 GTB series was well under way. *Hilary A. Raab, Jr.*

carrozzerie during the run of the 250 GT highlights Ferrari's massive expansion at the time. It also points out the small scale on which the *carrozzerie* operated, as no one *carrozzeria* was able to support Ferrari's new workload. In fact, Ferrari's main designer and coachbuilder, Pinin Farina, grew out of its shop in Turin and expanded by building new works in the Turinese town of Grugliasco. The first year of operations at Grugliasco was 1959, a peak year of 250 GT production. Coachbuilding techniques at Grugliasco were modernized—and standardized—by the use of templates for controlling the handmade bodies, now constructed on assembly lines.

While the assembly lines were rolling with the series cars at Ferrari, the factory was continuing with limited runs of one-off styling and engineering exercises. The 410 and 400 Superamericas, 500 Superfast and 365 California, produced in a total of 131 cars from 1956 to 1967, kept alive the Ferrari tradition on another front.

The Ferrari-Fiat marriage

From the mid 1960s through the 1970s, Ferrari continued to expand. On January 11, 1964, the 330 GT was unveiled at Maranello on the same day as a new wing at the factory was opened. From there, the factory built on to the workshops and offices, and added the *mensa* cafeteria in a giant restructuring in 1969–70. The effect was another doubling in total size of the Maranello works. The workforce also doubled from the estimated 500 workers in 1965 to 1,000 in 1970, reaching 1,643 in 1980. During this period, car production continued to grow as well, climbing to over 1,000 cars built annually in 1971 and topping the 2,000 mark in 1979.

The major force behind this expansion was Fiat.

The story behind Fiat's partial purchase of Ferrari began years before. In 1960, Ferrari, one of the world's smallest auto makers, purchased the Italian offices of Ford of Europe in Bologna, then the world's second largest auto maker. Beyond being a public relations coup, the move was more ironic than practical. And indeed, Ferrari sold the building soon after.

In 1963, Enzo Ferrari changed face and began to court Ford of America as a possible purchaser of his whole company. Ferrari made his approach to Ford of America in an arcane manner befitting a medieval lord: he spoke to Ford of Europe, headquartered in Cologne, Germany, through the German consul in Milan. The asking price for

Ferrari, Maranello, circa 1968
The main raised assembly lines with the V–6 engined Dinos to the left and the V–12 engined 330 GTC cars at right. This was the end of the line for the assembly process and the cars were still awaiting wheels and tires, the last items to be added before they were rolled down the ramp for testing and finishing. *Museo dell'Automobile Carlo Biscaretti di Ruffia*

Automobili Ferrari SEFAC S.p.A. was $18 million. Negotiations with Ford proposed two jointly owned companies: Ferrari-Ford, concentrating on racing and controlled by Enzo Ferrari as majority shareholder; and Ford-Ferrari, producing road cars and supervised by Ford.

Why Ferrari made this move has been disputed. Following the death of his and Laura's son Dino in 1956, speculation was that Enzo Ferrari became disillusioned with automobile manufacturing. It also seems possible that Ferrari was uninterested in or perhaps overwhelmed by the new assembly lines and larger-scale production at Maranello, and wished to distill his company back to his original passion of racing. Either way, in the end the sale to Ford fell through.

Six years later, on June 21, 1969, Fiat became half-owner of Ferrari. At the time, press reports deciphered the sale as Fiat's bailing out of Ferrari in a period of financial woes. Other accounts dispute this, however, stating that Ferrari was not faced with economic troubles but wanted to ensure the survival of his company and to continue in the expensive sport of racing.

Bob Wallace was at Lamborghini at the time of Fiat's partial purchase of Ferrari, and he remembered it as an important event for the Maranello factory for several reasons. Although Ferruccio Lamborghini had started his works at Sant'Agata Bolognese with brand-new state-of-the-art machine tools, dynamometers and buildings, Fer-

Ferrari factory, Maranello, 1972
Another view of the twin assembly lines showed a 246 GT and 365 GTC/4 receiving final work before road testing. The first assembly line did not have ramps to roll the cars down, relying on an overhead hoist to lower them to the floor from some five to six feet above. One technique that did not change on the line was the use of workers' muscle to push the cars forward along the runways. *Hilary A. Raab, Jr.*

Ferrari factory, Maranello, 1972
Alongside the twin raised assembly lines, a makeshift line constructed Fiat Dinos for Fiat. Painted and partially assembled Coupe and Spyder bodies arrived at Maranello from Carrozzeria Bertone and Pininfarina, respectively. Ferrari V-6 engines and drivetrains were then added to finish the cars. In an ironic about-face, Fiat had earlier constructed the first Ferrari 206 GT Dinos at its factories. *Hilary A. Raab, Jr.*

Ferrari factory, Maranello, 1972
The end of the makeshift Fiat Dino assembly line. Over the years, Ferrari set up numerous such lines to produce specials and limited-run cars, such as the later 288 GTO and the F40. In the background was the service department for test cars. After a test run, the cars would come back for modifications or maintenance before being delivered to the finishing room. In the late 1970s, a separate building was constructed for the service and finishing departments. *Hilary A. Raab, Jr.*

rari had been laboring on with largely the same equipment he had started with in 1946. Lamborghini had his lucrative tractor empire to support him; now Ferrari had a firm foundation as well in Fiat.

Wallace: "Ferrari stood on his own feet for many, many years. He had to make the factory pay for itself, and he had to make do with lots of old machine tools and other equipment. After Fiat bought into Ferrari, the factory slowly became one of the most advanced factories of its type in the world.

"Ferrari had struggled for quite a while. In the 1960s, the amount of money Ferrari had to spend working on pollution controls and emission laws left him no money for R and D or racing. Without Fiat he wouldn't have survived."

Through the years following the Ferrari-Fiat marriage, Fiat may have had a greater influence on the way Ferraris were built than on the design and direction of the cars themselves. While the 206/246 GT and the 308 GTB series blossomed following Fiat's entrance, Maranello had already sown the seeds for larger-scale sports car production with the 330 and 275 GT series; Fiat's capital made this possible. Inside the factory in 1989, Ferrari workers punctuated descriptions of their jobs with comments that "Fiat constructed this building" or "Fiat supplied these machines."

Fiat had a hand in supporting Ferrari through the tough economic times of the 1970s. On one side came the OPEC oil crisis, which was dooming sports cars sales. On another side came Italian labor unrest through much of the 1970s, culminating in intensity with the *Brigate Rosse,* or Red Brigades. The ongoing labor strikes slowed production in factories across Italy.

Handbuilding Ferraris in the 1990s

Many things changed at Ferrari from 1946 to 1990. The physical size of the factory work space grew by more than ten times and the labor force increased from 100 workers in 1943 to 1,281 in 1988. Meanwhile, car construction climbed from three finished cars in the first year to more than 4,000 in 1988. In 1990, the Maranello and Modena works included 148,000 square meters, or 1,593,000 square feet, of area; 72,000 square meters, or 775,000 square feet, of that was covered as factory shops.

The way in which those cars were built changed as well. The first cars were fabricated atop jigs one by one, component by component. In 1951–52, road car construction was separated from race car construction, although the work technique was largely the same. In 1958–59, the first assembly line was erected with an overhead runway for building some ten cars at a time; a second runway was built circa 1960.

Following page
Ferrari factory, Maranello, 1989
In the 1980s, the old twin raised assembly lines were removed and dual assembly lines on the floor replaced them. The 308 GTB series quickly filled the lines with Mondial production slotted in. By 1989, the first 1990 model 348s were well under construction, blended with the last 328s. The benefit of the former raised runways was that workers on the floor could assemble the undercarriage at the same time as workers on the raised portion dropped in the engine. The modernized line had automated overhead hoists that lifted the car for several stages of the assembly operation.

Ferrari factory, Maranello, 1979
The twin assembly lines continued production into the 1980s, here with the replacement for the 246 GT, the 308 GT4, and the replacement for the V–12 front engined GT cars, the 512 BB. *Hilary A. Raab, Jr.*

Ferrari factory, Maranello, circa 1972
The holding room for bodies fresh from the *carrozzerie* contained early 365 GT4 BB and 365 GT4 2+2 cars from Pininfarina and in the background, late Scaglietti 246 GT and GTS Dinos. The process of forming the bodywork at the two coachbuilders and then trucking the bodies to Ferrari for final assembly continued. The bodies arrived painted and with electrics assembled, sitting on rolling jigs. With the erection of a paint shop at Maranello in 1978, Scaglietti cars were painted at Ferrari; Pininfarina cars were still painted at the Grugliasco works. *Hilary A. Raab, Jr.*

Ferrari Versus Lamborghini: The Great Challenge

Legend has it that Ferruccio Lamborghini was so dismayed with his Ferrari that he threw down the gauntlet, issuing his challenge to build a better *granturismo* automobile.

Who won the challenge has been the debate now for two decades, but on one point, Lamborghini must be thanked. By constructing his mid-engined Miura as a road car, he spurred the conservative Ferrari to a new era in road car thinking. The same thanks must go to the racing Jaguars for their disc brakes and to others throughout the years.

Behind the scenes, Lamborghini and Ferrari were waging another war and on similar fronts. This was a war of economics, in keeping the companies alive in the market—and in keeping the factory and its tooling up to date based on the capital at hand.

Bob Wallace moved from the Ferrari race shop to the new Sant'Agata Bolognese works at the start of the Lamborghini era. He remembered well the differences in factory working conditions and techniques in building the two competing car lines: "In 1962–63, Lamborghini started

Ferrari factory, Maranello, circa 1955
Enzo Ferrari was especially proud of his modern machine tools shop, as this factory promotional photograph displayed. Many of these same machine tools were still in use more than a decade later until Fiat's partial purchase of Ferrari allowed for new machinery. Meanwhile, in the nearby town of Sant'Agata Bolognese, Ferruccio Lamborghini was mounting his *granturismo* challenge from a brand-new purpose-built factory equipped with the latest in tooling and Japanese-style assembly lines. *Road & Track*

from scratch. He had no obligations to use old machine tools and buildings. He could afford to buy brand new equipment and buy the best. Lamborghini had the very wealthy industrial tractor complex behind him that was already established.

"Ferrari did not have millions of dollars to buy everything brand new, and he had to make do with lots of old machine tools." In fact, many of the machine tools that Ferrari had started with in 1946 were still being soldiered on into the 1960s, Wallace recalled.

To build cars, Lamborghini built a new factory. The huge glass-and-steel works towered above the town's stone and wood houses and businesses. Ferrari used the brick-and-timber works he had built during the war years as a home for his machine tools fabrication plant. At Lamborghini, an assembly line was erected from almost the beginning with an overhead runway, the likes of which Ferrari did not have for some twelve years after starting car construction.

Lamborghini was also a student of assembly line construction of tractors and now cars. He had visited Soichiro Honda's modern works in Japan and had unabashedly copied organizational and systematic techniques to his Italian plants. Thus, while Ferrari was making the transition from building cars atop jigs, as in a race shop, to building them on an early crude assembly line, Lamborghini was miles ahead.

Lamborghini started off building cars in a tiered organizational approach: subcomponents were assembled at separate assembly lines and then passed on to the main line, where they were simply bolted into the car, according to Wallace. At Ferrari, the assembly job was more time-consuming and less efficient, taking place primarily on the single line—the cars waited while the work was performed. The results were probably the same at the two factories in terms of hands-on attention to detail, just different in terms of work technique and organization.

Assembly of engines followed a similar pattern. Ferrari V–12s were usually built by an individual worker, while Lamborghini's were put together by a team, again with subcomponents preassembled.

With the arrival of Fiat came a major restructuring of car building at Ferrari, but the changes in organization and financing were slow. "It took six years for Fiat money to trickle down to the finished product," Wallace said.

All in all, Lamborghini was probably one step ahead of the times in organization and Ferrari was probably one step behind. Ferrari wouldn't reach the stage of organization at which Lamborghini began for another five to ten years.

Lamborghini's financial foundation not only provided capital to begin work with, but helped smooth over rough economic times. With about 1,000 tractors rolling off the assembly lines annually, the car manufacturing was almost a hobby.

For Ferrari, the bottom line on the car construction was the bottom line for everything. "Ferrari has to be admired for keeping going, keeping the factory running, continuing to race," Wallace stated. Where Lamborghini was backing his cars with sturdy tractor sales, Ferrari was backing his racing with the vagaries of the *granturismo* car market. Salvation came for Ferrari in the form of Fiat, Wallace maintained.

One other explanation for discrepancies in car construction between Lamborghini and Ferrari was the philosophies of the two men. Ferrari wanted to build racing cars, and it's possible that the road car factory did not always receive the attention from him that it needed or deserved. For Lamborghini, the road cars were the focus. As Wallace stated, "Ferrari existed to go racing. Lamborghini did not even want to hear of the word being mentioned."

In the early 1970s, two makeshift lines were set up to assemble Fiat Dino 2.4 liter cars. Similar lines were used in the 1980s to construct the special series cars, such as the 288 GTO.

In 1990, the factory boasted four complete assembly lines. On the two central lines, the V–8 engined road cars were produced with automated overhead hoists moving the cars. A sophisticated system for supplying components to the assemblers ran throughout the factory from the foundry to the engine builders, and beyond to subcontractors

Ristorante Cavallino, Maranello, 1972
The former restaurant building prior to the rebuilding. *Hilary A. Raab, Jr.*

Ristorante Cavallino, Maranello, 1989
Across via Abetone Inferiore from the main gate of the Ferrari factory stood the Ferrari restaurant. In the 1950s, the Cavallino Bianco bar was located on the site, offering traditional northern Italian country inn food. With the refurbishing of the building, the cuisine was dramatically upgraded, making this one of the best restaurants in the area.

throughout Italy and, indeed, the world. Testarossas were built on a smaller line to one side; F40s were constructed on the other side of the central lines on a makeshift assembly line. At the start of 1990, Ferrari was completing twelve to fourteen cars daily: eight 348s; three Mondial t's; two Testarossas; and 0.8 to two F40s. The exclusiveness of a Ferrari in the 1990s was set more by its price tag than by the limited number of cars.

Above all, the definition of a handmade automobile evolved. As of 1990, Ferraris were still largely handmade cars, but in a different way than they were handmade cars in the 1950s. The difference lay in the technique, the tools, the system and the scale of construction.

In 1950, the mechanical components were fabricated for a car within the same workshop as the car was assembled; in 1990, components were fabricated within the same factory, but in a different wing

owing to the size of the works. In both 1950 and 1990, machine tools were operated hands-on by workers, although some machines were automated in 1990, requiring different expertise. Wrenches and screwdrivers were still in use in all aspects of assembling cars, but in 1990 electric power tools were used more frequently, although they were still hand-held and operated.

The system of assembling a car probably changed the most, and this was because of the growing scale of production over the years. In 1950, the worker who fabricated a component may have also been the one to assemble that component onto the car. In 1990, this was no longer feasible: one worker was fabricating the component while another worker assembed it. Assembly has had to become more systematized and, in the course, less personal.

The detailed work on the F40 line was a step back in time. Twelve

Ferrari factory, Maranello, 1989
Building the F40 V–8. Testarossa and F40 engine assembly at Ferrari was typically a one-person job, but teams of two workers usually built the production V–8 engines.

Ferrari factory, Maranello, 1989
Ferrari fabricated and upholstered its own seats and interiors for the Testarossa and V–8 production cars within the factory. An area was walled off for the assembly, with cutting machines and expansive worktables for trimming the leather hides from patterns. Rows of workers at sewing machines and others cutting and shaping the foam inserts finished the operation.

Ferrari factory, Maranello, 1989
Initial steps in assembling an F40 V–8 engine. While the engines for the Testarossa and the V–8 production cars were built in designated areas with timed stages for construction, the limited run of some 900 F40 engines were constructed off in a corner of the factory.

Ferrari factory, Maranello, 1989
Coke was it at Ferrari as well, although most workers on break chose coffee from the Zanussi vending machine. Coffee, in all its forms from espresso to cappuccino, was available from the machine with a *gettone* token, which was purchased from the factory. These vending machines were situated within the works between the Green Giants automated milling machines and the sector where heads were polished. In the background within the glass walls was the metallurgy lab with its computerized equipment for testing the alloy make-up of cast components. Note the ubiquitous bicycle, used as transportation everywhere inside the factory.

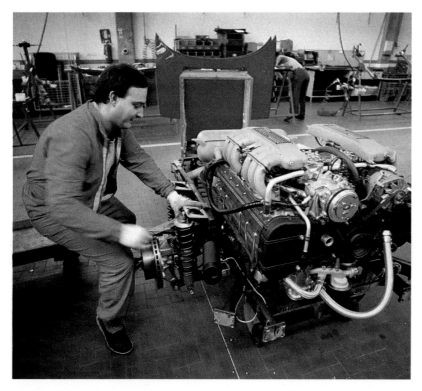

Ferrari factory, Maranello, 1989
Off to one side of the Testarossa line, a flat-twelve engine was rolled into position atop a wheeled trolley. Sitting on the tail end of a crowbar, the worker compressed the shock-absorber-and-spring unit and fit it into the mount on the engine unit.

workers did all the assembly, moving from inserting Plexiglas windows to bolting on turbochargers, and at times making extensive modifications to components to fit them to the chassis. All time-consuming labor-intensive work, much as Ferrari construction was in the 1950s.

Other things changed at Ferrari as well. Spokespeople stated that in 1990, eighty percent of all components were made within Ferrari versus among the legions of subcontractors. Looking at the number of components arriving through the Maranello delivery gates makes this hard to believe: Pirelli and Bridgestone tires, Momo steering wheels, CEV electrics, and Weber/Marelli fuel injection systems, as well as non-Ferrari wheels, windshield glass, leather upholstery hides and details such as rubber weather stripping, carpeting, gauges—the list goes on. Still, only ten percent of the Maranello works was given over to assembling cars as of 1990.

Ferrari factory, Maranello, 1989
With the shocks in place, the retaining bolts were torqued using an electric socket drive. The waiting Testarossa body sat behind.

One other change is a sign of the times and of Ferrari's history. From the 1950s to the early 1970s, Ferrari road cars were painted in a variety of colors from deep maroon to black to dark blue; only the race cars were painted in the Italian racing red. Indeed, many early road car body designs were made to be painted in more subtle, luxurious colors to emphasize the lines; painted in red, those same designs appeared overweight, heavy and dull. But through the years, red has come to symbolize Ferrari on both road and race cars, and with the advent of the 365 GT4 BB and the 308 GTB series, red became the production color. In 1989, fully eighty percent of the cars being built at Maranello were ordered in red.

Ferrari automobile production, 1947-1990

Year	Production	Total to date	Year	Production	Total to date
1947	3	3	1969	619	6,884
1948	5	8	1970	928	7,812
1949	21	29	1971	1,246	9,058
1950	26	55	1972	1,844	10,902
1951	33	88	1973	1,772	12,674
1952	44	132	1974	1,436	14,110
1953	57	189	1975	1,337	15,447
1954	58	247	1976	1,426	16,873
1955	61	308	1977	1,798	18,671
1956	81	389	1978	1,939	20,610
1957	113	502	1979	2,221	22,831
1958	183	685	1980	2,470	25,301
1959	248	933	1981	2,565	27,866
1960	306	1,239	1982	2,209	30,075
1961	441	1,680	1983	2,366	32,441
1962	493	2,173	1984	2,842	35,283
1963	598	2,771	1985	3,119	38,402
1964	654	3,425	1986	3,640	42,042
1965	740	4,165	1987	3,902	45,944
1966	665	4,830	1988	4,001	49,945
1967	706	5,536	1989	3,821	53,766
1968	729	6,265	1990	approx. 4,000	

Ferrari factory, Maranello, 1989
Dwarfed between the overhead body and the monstrous flat-twelve engine, a worker backed the engine into place in the middle of the car. By himself, this worker took care of the most important portion of the car's assembly.

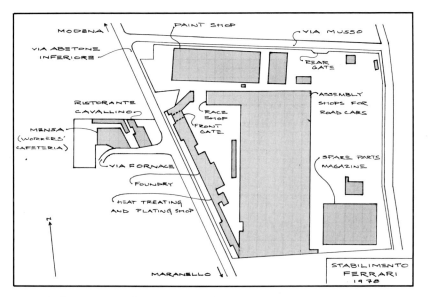

Layout of the Ferrari factory, 1978. The major additions in the late 1970s included the paint shop, transferred from Carrozzeria Scaglietti in Modena, and the spare parts facility, located at the lower right.

Number of Ferrari employees, 1939-1990

	Year	Employees
Modena		
	1939–40	approx. 40
Maranello		
	1943	approx. 100
	1946	140
	1950	200
	1955	250
	1960	370
	1965	approx. 500
	1970	1,000
	1975	approx. 1,200
	1980	1,643
	1985	1,715
	1988	1,727

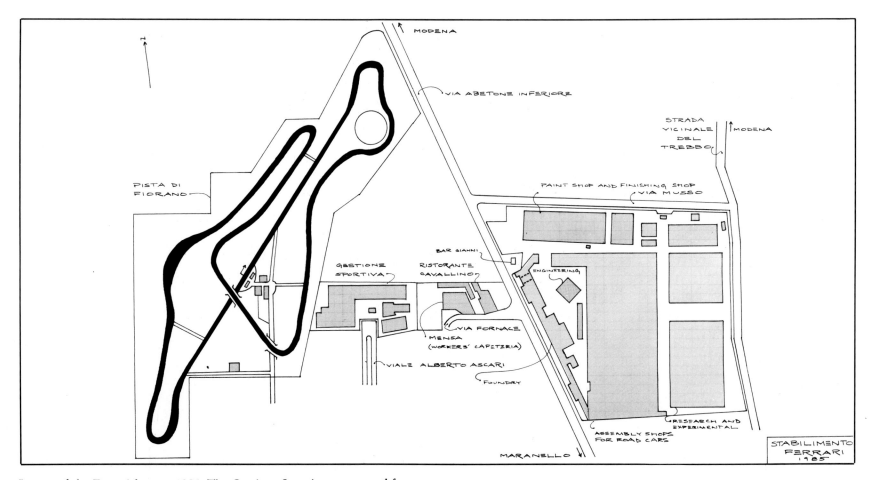

Layout of the Ferrari factory, 1985. The Gestione Sportiva was moved from within the factory walls to a site neighboring the workers cafeteria, albeit in the parish of Fiorano. The test track had been laid out previously.

Ferrari factory, Maranello, 1989
Over the past few years since the factory's waiting-room-cum-showroom was added, a variety of cars had been on display, including the F40, Michele Alboreto's Formula One car and the 1950 Tipo 166 Formula Two racer shown here. A case of Ferrari models lined the right wall. Only a few chairs were available and these were rarely used; most visitors stood to admire the cars. The doors hidden in the wall at left led to the factory courtyard; the door in the far wall led to the administration offices. A door in the right wall led to a conference room and the office headquarters for the Ferrari Club Italia.

Number of Ferrari employees by department, 1978–1988

Year	Ferrari Maranello	Gestione Sportiva	Scaglietti Modena	Total
1978				1,398
1979				1,576
1980				1,643
1981				1,606
1982				1,599
1983				1,599
1984	1,154	194	257	1,605
1985	1,246	198	271	1,715
1986	1,203	204	309	1,716
1987	1,293	216	266	1,775
1988	1,281	227	220	1,728

Ferrari, Maranello, 1989
Front gates of the factory in the 1990s, off via Abetone Inferiore.

The Prototype Junkyard

Enzo Ferrari was never kind to last year's race cars. The adage went that the two-year-old racer was nothing but junk. A race was won—or a lesson was learned.

Photographs in the mid 1950s showed a sorry sight: the great Lancia D50 racers that Ferrari had inherited languishing in an open shed behind the factory. The pile of cars was parked forever, waiting only for the metal scrapper.

The discarding of prototypes, old racers, specials, projects or failed show cars has existed among the Italian car and motorcycle makers since their founding. Lamborghini used to abandon its cars on the other side of the factory walls, leaving them to rust and decay. If the vehicles were lucky, they were divided up and born again as other specials or racers.

As of 1990, Ferrari had realized the value of the old racers and prototypes, and these were no longer simply thrown out to the junkyard or the first person with money in hand. That practice ended not so very long ago, however. In the late 1970s, the prototypes, bodywork bucks and one-off specials were still consigned to junk.

Ferrari factory, Maranello, 1979
As late as 1979, the factory was still discarding unwanted prototypes, specials and one-offs after they had served their purpose—a practice seemingly traditional to Italian car and motorcycle manufacturers. Languishing in the center of this photograph was the 1977 model 308 GTB Speciale, chassis number 23611, converted by Pininfarina with riveted-on aluminum race-styled bodywork as a styling exercise. Elements of the design, from the roof spoiler to the extra foglights, were incorporated into the 288 GTO and 328s. The car was displayed in this "deliberately unfinished" form at the 1977 Geneva Show before being cast out. *Hilary A. Raab, Jr.*

Ferrari factory, Maranello, 1979
The discarded prototypes received the same respect due used oil cans. The car at far left was mid-engined but difficult to identify in this state—probably a 365 GT4 BB. The 308 GTB Speciale was flanked by an early unfinished 308 GTS—possibly a prototype or a production car that didn't pass testing. In any case, no one even bothered to roll up the side windows before junking the car. In the background was a factory parking lot for employees, filled with the usual Fiats, Alfa Romeos and Peugeots. The field was later covered by additional factory buildings. *Hilary A. Raab, Jr.*

Ferrari factory, Maranello, 1979
Alongside the 308 GTS sat the styling mockup for the first Bertone 308 GT4. The body appeared to be of steel, the frame was of wooden boards. Note the indent on the hood for the Dino badge. To the right was a similar Pininfarina 365 GT4 BB styling mockup with rough metal bodywork covering a wooden frame. *Hilary A. Raab, Jr.*

Ferrari factory, Maranello, 1979
That the 308 GT4 was initially produced as a Dino is well-known; here was a mockup for the 308 GTB series with an indent on the hood for the Dino logo as well. The styling of the GTB with its updated and angularized rendering of the 246 GT was the first hint of a successor. This simple hood indent gave a further clue as to official factory plans for the GTB series before introduction in 1975. The early nose design differed from that on the final production cars, but most other elements from the hoodlines to the wheel arches and rear tail lip were used. This mockup rested in peace between the 365 GT4 BB and an unfinished 308 GT4—obviously not meant to be seen. *Hilary A. Raab, Jr.*

Ferrari factory, Maranello, 1989
The central courtyard of the factory was entered through the famous square archway. Once upon a time, this courtyard was filled with poplar trees and cobbled pavement, the site of many a Ferrari press introduction of the latest race cars. In 1981, the tall square building was constructed in the center of the courtyard, housing the Ferrari design and engineering studios. Portions of the old Modena-yellow factory were visible through the trees surrounding the building. Three flags flew over Ferrari: left, the Italian *tricolore;* center, the Ferrari flag with the prancing horse on a field of yellow; and right, the light blue United Nations banner.

Ferrari, Maranello, 1989
Rear gates of the factory opened off via Musso. Test cars came and went through these gates, stopping to sign out at the guardhouse. Trucks carrying components from proprietary manufacturers also used these gates.

Ferrari factory, Maranello, 1989
The famous noontime rush of workers from the assembly lines, foundry and technical offices within the factory, through the square archway, across via Abetone Inferiore, past Ristorante Cavallino and around the corner to the factory *mensa* cafeteria. Workers dash from the assembly lines and offices in staggered spurts to queue up for lunch. This was the main entrance to the factory, with a small visitor parking lot just within the gates. To the right was the main entrance desk and the waiting room. Blue overalls were for workers in the *fabbrica,* "factory"; red overalls were for *servizio,* "service mechanics"; brown overalls were for *controllo di qualità,* "quality control inspectors"; white was for *chimecca,* "lab personnel."

Ferrari, Maranello, 1989
Entrance to the workers *mensa* cafeteria behind the Ristorante Cavallino on via Fornace. Workers from the main factory and the race shop ate at the cafeteria, arriving in shifts to queue up at the counter. Food was good, according to assembly line workers, with a choice of pasta, entrée and desserts everyday. After-meal espresso was found next door to the factory at the Bar Gianni.

Ferrari factory, Maranello, 1989
Neighboring the main factory entrance on via Abetone Inferiore was the Bar Gianni, ideal for an after-meal espresso or ice cream. On a sunny day, these assembly line workers pulled chairs out to read the newspaper's pink sports section or to watch the passing traffic, girls and *prova* Ferraris. The main door of the bar sported a sticker from most every Ferrari club in the world, and a rear spoiler from a Formula One car hung inside, signed by the famous *corridori*.

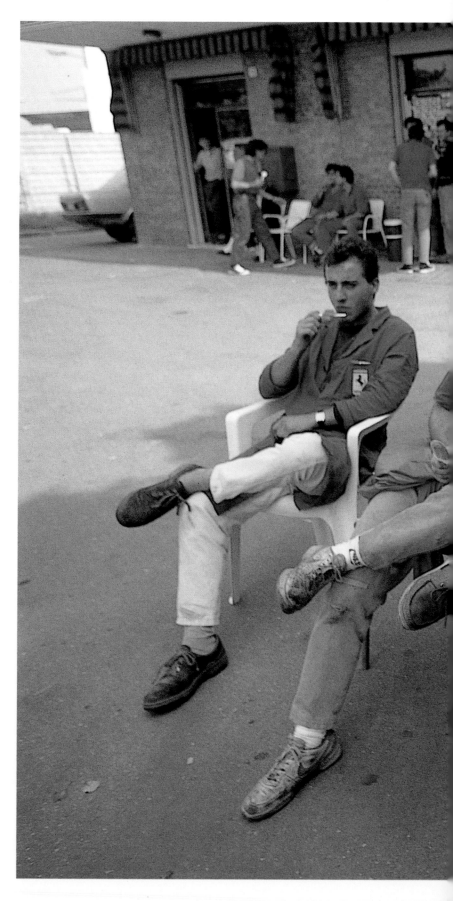

Chapter 3

Le Carrozzerie

From Tree Stumps to World-Famous Designwork

In 1958, American Mark Wallach visited Carrozzeria Scaglietti on the outskirts of Modena. Wallach, as Le Mans team manager for Ed Hugus' *scuderia* of Ferrari and Porsche racers, raced four times at the twenty-four-hour endurance event. His interest in Ferrari was intimate; his most striking remembrance of the Scaglietti workshop was auditory: "The shop was pure noise." Here was a small, nondescript garage packed with workers in dusty overalls building beautiful flowing bodywork for Ferrari. One group of workers used hammers to

Carrozzeria Scaglietti, Modena, 1989
Robotic welders worked on an early 348 steel body. The twin machines attacked each side of the bodywork following a preset computerized program. Scaglietti workers merely positioned the body, punched a series of buttons and stood back to watch, out of range of the spray of sparks.

Carrozzeria Scaglietti, Modena, 1963
Carrozzeria Scaglietti moved to these new, expanded works along via Emilia Est in 1959. The former works had been housed nearby, behind a Fiat concessionaire, and the coachbuilder divided its work between building racing car bodies for Ferrari and repairing crash-damaged Fiats. With this new shop, Scaglietti would concentrate on both road and race Ferraris. *Robert Bodin Collection*

pound aluminum panels into shape with tree trunks as the molds. The maestro panelbeater smoothed the panels atop a steel planishing table. Within the confines of the garage, it was absolute cacophony. "They had no machines in the shop," Wallach remembered, "just workers pounding away with hammers, and you heard it the minute you walked in the door: pure noise!"

If, as Enzo Ferrari once said, the engine is the soul of a Ferrari automobile, then the bodywork provides the car's corporeal body, telling of its function in its form. Ferrari never had its own bodyshop at Maranello; only after the 1970–71 purchase of Scaglietti with the aid of Fiat did Ferrari have a body builder directly under its aegis. With Enzo Ferrari's well-known iron hand ruling quality control, it's interesting to note the freedom and trust he allowed his favored bodyshops in forming the image his cars presented to the world.

The first Ferrari Tipo 125 was clothed with bodywork by the prestigious Carrozzeria Touring Superleggera on via Lodovico de Breme in Milan. The second to body a Ferrari was Stabilimenti Farina; founded in 1905 in Milan, it was the oldest bodyshop, before the days of Carrozzeria Pinin Farina. Since then, Ferraris were the most sought after chassis to be clothed by Bertone, Zagato, Michelotti, Vignale, Ghia, Drogo, Boano, Ellena, Fantuzzi, Fontana, Abarth and several

Carrozzeria Scaglietti, Modena, 1955
The coachwork for the Ferrari of Italian filmmaker Roberto Rossellini was constructed in the workroom of Scaglietti. The car, 375 MM serial number 0402AM, was in the body design planning stage here, as the right front fender wheel cutout was shaped different from the left—and neither shape was used.

The top, however, had already assumed the shape it would wear on the finished car. Ferrari sports racers appeared in the background of this photo, and a Fiat 500 underwent crash damage repair. Sergio Scaglietti was at center, wearing suit and tie. *Bob Gurr, courtesy Dean Batchelor*

others over the years. But the two most famous and prolific Ferrari bodyshops have remained those of Pinin Farina and Scaglietti.

Italian coachbuilding: "Crude artistry"

Much of the Italian coachbuilders' worldwide fame rests on the shoulders of English journalists. Following World War II, the austerity programs in England rationed gasoline, and shortages of food were commonplace. Luxury items were remembrances of prewar days, and even the first postwar British automobiles were built primarily for export to less war-weary countries such as the United States. The picture was much the same in postfascist Italy, where several industrious workers had found bombed-out prewar automobiles, cut away the tired bodywork and hammered together new, stylish bodies using whatever material was at hand. The British motoring journalists heard tell of these "new" cars, applied for gas coupons, and traveled south to the sunshine, good food, wine and women of Italy—and along the way stopped in to report on the fabulous doings of these unknown *carrozzerie* and their *combinazione,* "combination," cars. This press brought fame to more than one obscure coachbuilder.

In the 1950s, as in the 1990s, Italy was a land of small body works located in garages and workshops set off on back streets in every city. In the early days of the automobile—and in the days of the horsedrawn carriage before—the *carrozzerie* crafted unique coachwork on hire. They supplied both elegant town cars for the rich and lightweight aluminum bodies for racers, notably the Zagato-bodied Alfa Romeos that Ferrari raced in the 1920s. Customers could drive their cars into a

Carrozzeria Scaglietti, Modena, 1955
Another view of the Rossellini 375 MM showed the rod body mockup early in the design stage. The fenderline ran from the rear over the front tire—and was held above the tire by a C-section piece as makeshift support. An uncut rod also lay across the hood space, running through the cockpit. *Bob Gurr, courtesy Dean Batchelor*

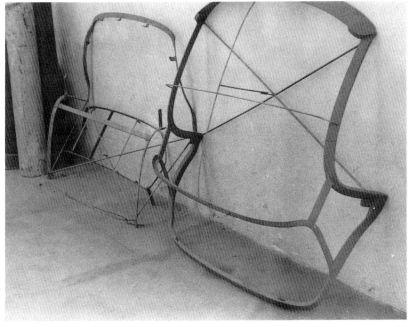

Carrozzeria Scaglietti, Modena, 1958
Molds such as these 250 GT roof molds resting against a wall at Scaglietti were formed by welding together small-diameter iron welding rods. The body panels—in this case, roofs—were hand-beaten on tree stumps and then held up onto these molds to test fitment. If a contour was off, the panel went back to the tree stump for further pounding. When complete, the panel would be spot-welded to the rest of the car's bodywork. *Mark Wallach*

Carrozzeria Scaglietti, Modena, 1958
A series of three 250 GT Spyder California cars was bodied in the *carrozzeria's* workshop. This was largely the extent of Carrozzeria Scaglietti's shop before the move to the new works in 1959. In the foreground, the burnished finish of the 250 GT Spyder California fender was apparent. In the background, note the rounded stand for shaping metal; behind the far car, a worker was forming a hood, complete with scoop. *Mark Wallach*

coachbuilder and have the stock body replaced with a special creation to their order, or purchase a chassis-engine combination from an auto maker and have it clothed by a *carrozzeria*. Coachbuilders also did more routine work converting ambulances, hearses and trucks. *Road & Track* reported that in 1956, the price for custom bodying of a car by Scaglietti ranged around $3,000—complex designs could run up to $6,000. At the same time, cars from Maranello cost around $9,500. In relation, the price of this handwork was low, as workers were abundant and inexpensive.

The *carrozzerie* built bodies following the Italian school of panelbeating. Hammers, sandbags and tree stumps were used to create body panels, allowing bodies to be composed quickly and easily. Alterations or modifications could be made in moments and from body to body.

The English coachbuilders of the time had perfected the so-called English wheel, using a roller and form held in a large vise to work the metal into shape. The English wheel required much more exacting and time-consuming work; it was also more gentle with the formed metal, whereas the Italians' panelbeating tended to work-harden the material. In Germany, construction of bodywork for sports cars such as the Mercedes-Benz 300 SL relied on modern presses to stamp out panels. The presses created uniformly perfect panels, but were expensive and only economical with large production runs. English wheels and machine presses were not present in the Italian *carrozzerie*, which stood behind their panelbeating technique, a technique that had changed little from the hammering of suits of armor for medieval knights.

Later on, Italian coachbuilders also used power hammers, machines blending the concept of the English wheel with that of the panelbeat-

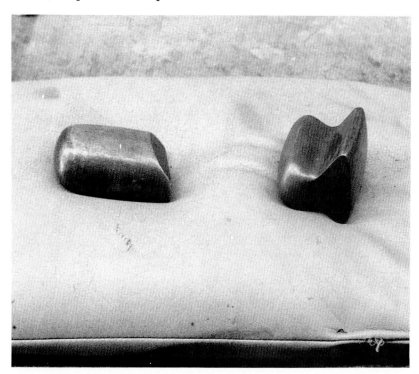

Steel dollies such as these were held by hand on the back side of a panel while a metalworking hammer was used on the front. The different faces of the dollies provided different shapes to the finished metal. The dollies sat atop a leather-covered sandbag, which provided a rest for the hand holding the dollies. Working in this way, the panelbeater was a sort of human stamping machine.

The heavy steel planishing table provided solid backing for finishing work on hand-beaten body panels. Behind it stood a dolly mounted atop a stand. Panels were set against the dolly and hammered to form curves and contours. These were the tools of former Carrozzeria Fissore panelbeater, Andre De Stepfanis, who as of 1989 was working at Scott Restorations in Panorama City, California.

ers. The electric-powered hammer pounded the metal into shape using metalworking forms. Carrozzeria Touring had such power hammers as early as 1941, but the machines did not arrive at other coachbuilding shops almost a decade later.

The working techniques at the various Italian coachbuilders in the early 1950s can best be described as crude artisanship. And these techniques changed little from the first Touring-bodied Tipo 166 cars of 1947 up through the last 365 GTB/4 Daytonas of 1973.

Carrozzeria Scaglietti, Modena, 1958
The black frame of this 250 GT Spyder California came from the frame maker, probably Gilco of Milan. Carrozzeria Scaglietti workers then formed the underbody around the frame. The frame and the bodywork were of steel and the body was typically connected to the chassis by welding. *Mark Wallach*

Carrozzeria Scaglietti, Modena, 1958
Looking forward from the rear of the 250 GT Spyder California, one saw that the gas tank was placed between the ladder-frame rails at bottom. The clamps at right were commonly used to hold sheets of metal together while joining them, either with weld or rivets. *Mark Wallach*

Carrozzeria Scaglietti, Modena, 1958
This view showed the midsection of the 250 GT Spyder California, looking toward the rear wheels. The wheelwells were formed of steel sheets, riveted together and then welded to the rear tubework. Under the rocker panel, the zigzag network of steel tubing was visible. The curved bar across the top of the photo was the support for the rear bodywork; the steel panels would be rolled over the bar. *Mark Wallach*

Carrozzeria Scaglietti, Modena, 1958
This was the empty engine compartment of the 250 GT Spyder California. The vents to channel air from the outer body scoops were visible at center, along with the tubing to route the flow. Note the coils of electrical wiring and the brake cable. *Mark Wallach*

In 1956, *Road & Track* described a visit to Scaglietti. The reporter was amazed at the simplicity of working conditions and the beautiful work produced there. Scaglietti had been founded in 1951 by Sergio Scaglietti to craft special car bodies and to repair crash damage to the everyday Fiats. The magazine saw the first Scaglietti shop before the move in 1959 to the current works, and said that it had only about 2,700 square meters, or 29,000 square feet, of working area—much less than the average American auto dealership showroom had in 1990—with half used for body construction, the other half for customers' body restyling. For the custom work, Scaglietti built a sketchy wire framework around the car's chassis and formed the aluminum body panels to fit, as with the Roberto Rossellini Ferrari then being built. For series cars, such as the Ferrari Monzas in the shop, Scaglietti used a wire buck as a mold to form the panels on. The aluminum used was about 2 mm to 2.5 mm thick, thinner and substantially lighter in weight than that used in American metal panels of the time.

Material Shortages: Cinzano to the Rescue

One night in the late 1940s, a group of Carrozzeria Touring workers left the coachbuilding shop in their car or truck and began scouring the roadways around Milan. Coming upon a building, tree, telephone pole or signpost bearing one of the numerous metal advertising panels of the day, they stopped the vehicle, quickly and quietly unfastened the sign, stuffed it inside and drove away. The metal advertisements were hand-painted with stylish graphic designs for Pirelli tires, Lancia cars, Rumi motorcycles, cigarette brands and the like. Commonly one square meter in size, to the coachbuilders they represented one square meter of raw steel for bodywork. With a full load of signs, the workers returned home.

Such raiding parties in the dark of night were the result of the material shortages in Italy following World War II. The shortages were a curse to fledgling fabricators like Ferrari, the coachbuilders and the subcontracted suppliers. Many factories—Ferrari included, according to legend—were fortunate enough to buy up aluminum stock left over from the war's airplane manufacturers, such as Aer Macchi and Caproni. The purchases were often made through the Allied occupying forces, which had taken control of Italy following the defeat of Mussolini's fascist government. Again according to legend, some early Ferrari engine blocks were cast from this war surplus stock.

For other nonstressed components, manufacturers bought up or "collected" scrap metal from war wreckage, old cars and so on. Buying agents for factories searched Italy for scrap metal of any quality. Aluminum pistons from aircraft and automobile engines were melted down and recast, giving birth to a new pot metal jokingly named Pistonium.

The spoils of one sign-raiding party in the late 1940s turned up on an early Touring-bodied Tipo 166 Ferrari in Los Angeles. American restorer John Ling remembered servicing the 166 in Salvatore di Natale's former shop. While attending to the front suspension, he looked up underneath the front fender to see a dab of red paint showing through the black undercoating. Scratching off more of the undercoat revealed an aluminum display sign, handformed and butt-welded into the original bodywork. In flowing red script, the sign advertised Cinzano aperitif.

The preliminary shaping of the panel was done with panelbeating hammers and hand-sized steel forms called dollies for shaping the metal. There were three basic types of hammer faces: heavy-duty dome-faced bumping hammers for crude initial shaping; body hammers with a flat face on one side of the head and a round face on the other for planishing; and a smaller, round-faced pick hammer for finishing. Square-faced hammers were used to work metal into sharp corners, and point-faced hammers were used for confined spaces.

Dollies bore different faces from flat to dramatic curves as well. They were held in the palm of the hand as backing to form the panel profile. With the dolly behind the metal and using the hammer on the other side, the panelbeater was in effect a sort of human press tool.

A leather-covered sandbag was usually set on a table for backing while hammering. The panel was slowly worked over the dollies, hammered to displace metal and form the curves, then checked for fit on the mockup and corrected if need be. From there, the panel was beaten against an anvil to smooth out and perfect the final contours.

The bodywork was then attached in place to the light steel tube frame, which in turn was welded to the ladder-frame chassis. For fasteners, the *carrozzerie* used a potpourri of blind pop rivets, metal screws and bolts running into nuts tack-welded to the frame or other panels. Panels were usually spot butt-welded together.

Scaglietti workers appeared to worry little about corrosion between adjacent dissimilar metals—and why should they when the cars were being built primarily as racers that would be used for only a season or two? Thus, rivets, screws, and nuts and bolts were often used when connecting dissimilar metals, as between the aluminum body panels and the pot steel tubework. Where like metals were attached, as when several sections of aluminum were assembled into one fender or with steel-bodied road cars, weld was favored.

The steel body panels welded to the steel frames also presented problems with paint finishes. The panels were stressed along with the chassis, twisting as the frame twisted. The result was cracks running across the paintwork after only a few good drives.

The seams between body panels were hammer-welded for smoothness. Each seam was heated and pounded with a metalworking hammer, with a dolly hand-held on the opposite side of the metal to flatten the seam so it would not bulge. Fine-toothed metalworking files were then used to burnish the metal before priming and painting.

Carrozzeria Scaglietti, Modena, 1957

An aluminum-alloy-bodied 250 GT Scaglietti Comp. Berlinetta was constructed within the main workroom at the *carrozzeria*. Before the Ferrari assembly line got rolling, completed chassis were trucked from Maranello to the coachbuilders; the chassis were drivable, with engine, radiator, driveline, and wheels and tires all assembled. Note the paper simply laid over the engine to protect it. Here, a Scaglietti worker tack-hammered the roof section to the windshield pillar. Weld seams crisscrossed the car body and hammer dimples were visible everywhere on the metal. At far left, a worker was barely visible, forming the left headlamp into the fender with the aid of a metalworking hammer and a dolly, which was held to the inside of the body to shape the metal with pounding. Tools were scattered over the floor, a crowbar rested on the front fender, and metal tailings and shavings covered the ground. *Jesse Alexander*

Carrozzeria Scaglietti, Modena, 1957
Forming the headlamp pod for the alloy-bodied 250 GT Scaglietti Comp. Berlinetta. Three pieces of metal were rounded and then butt-welded together to form a circular tube. This tube was inserted into the headlamp hole in the front fender and then spot-welded in place. Numerous weld seams ran across the aluminum nose around the headlamp for all the different pieces of metal that made up this complex section of the car. In the background were welding gas tanks and at left was a heavy-duty steel planishing table for forming body panels. *Jesse Alexander*

The work at Scaglietti went quickly. From framework to finished body panels for a Ferrari, the process required about one week of work, according to *Road & Track*. The final fitting of the body and its mounting onto the chassis took a further three to four days.

Visiting Scaglietti in 1958, Mark Wallach recalled that the shop was connected to the back of a Fiat dealership, the two divided by Scaglietti's small paint booth. The workshop did repairs and some custom work for the dealership while also building many of the bodies for Ferrari's racing cars of the period. Upon Wallach's visit, twelve Ferrari chassis were being clothed in the shop. The works was a hubbub of noise and activity: numerous wire molds stacked in a jumble against the walls, a tangle of acetylene and oxygen lines for welding torches snaking across the floor underfoot.

Carrozzeria Scaglietti, Modena, 1962
Before priming and painting of the aluminum alloy, the series of panels making up the 250 GTO body were visible. Note the long seam running from the top of the front wheel arch all the way to the door, and the seam connecting the roof to the rear fender. In the end, the butt-welding would be smoothed over and covered with a talc and resin body filler to hide seam and rivet lines. Looking through the front wheel arch, the tube from the lower nose air vent was visible; this tube would direct air onto the front brakes. A tree stump and metalworking hammer were just visible at the lower right corner of the photograph. *Robert Bodin Collection*

Carrozzeria Scaglietti, Modena, 1962
The detail work on the 250 GTO's nose was tremendous—and time-consuming. The brake vents and foglight indents were all separate pieces of aluminum, handformed and spot-welded in place; the seams were then hammer-welded until they were almost invisible. The headlamp openings, nose vent and triple air vents were simply holes cut out of the bodywork with the metal bent back under the top side to form a clean edge. *Robert Bodin Collection*

Carrozzeria Scaglietti, Modena, 1962
Hammer dimples and hand file scratch marks were visible across the aluminum bodywork of the 250 GTO. Note the well-formed vent behind the rear wheel arch and the size of the spoiler. A metalworking anvil rested on the ground near the wall. *Robert Bodin Collection*

69

Superleggera Construction: The Technique and its Heritage

In the years preceding World War II, Carrozzeria Touring developed a unique style of lightweight automobile construction that revolutionized luxury and racing cars. Until the arrival of Touring's Superleggera, or superlight, body-chassis assembly, most street and race cars used chassis based on heavy steel support framework or even heavier wooden frames. Touring changed the way of thinking in the infant field of body-chassis engineering.

Touring's breakthrough came in the way the aluminum bodywork was attached to the chassis. By using an extensive framework of lightweight steel tubing that followed the form of the enveloping bodywork, the design did away with the heavy framework of former design styles. The steel tube superstructure was welded directly to the heavier-gauge steel tube ladder-frame chassis. Thus, the aluminum bodywork was not a stressed part of the frame.

Superleggera construction was first used on an Alfa Romeo racer in 1937; the first Ferraris so bodied were the Tipo 166 MM Touring *barchette* of 1948. Ferrari's early cars had relied on the more traditional—and suddenly old-fashioned—style of framework design, and the superlight construction was key to Ferrari's success. Basic elements of the Superleggera design were used in most of Ferrari's competition cars through the 250 GTO of 1963.

An examination of the bodywork and chassis construction techniques of two milestone Ferraris offers insight into the fabrication of the early cars and the relationship of the later cars to Ferrari's roots.

Tipo 166 MM Touring *barchetta* 0054 M

In 1989, Tipo 166 MM Touring *barchetta* serial number 0054 M was being rebuilt at Scott Grundfor's restoration shop in Panorama City, California. The car started life with Scuderia Ferrari and was later sold to Luigi Chinetti and Plisson in Paris. By the time Scott Restorations received the car, it had been outfitted with a four-cylinder Offenhauser race engine, among numerous other body and chassis modifications. Part of the ladder frame had been cut away to make room for the deep sump of the Offenhauser, and the body was in need of rejuvenation. With the body off the frame, panels were being remade atop a wooden mockup.

Although Enzo Ferrari's V–12 engine was radical for the era, his chassis was merely state of the art. It was a straightforward ladder-frame affair, as constructed in the early years by Gilco, Gilberto Colombo's works in Milan, which also built chassis for other racing *equipes* later on. The siderails of the Ferrari were made of 10 gauge oval-section high-carbon steel. At the tail, they were narrowed and angled upward. A seam along the underside from the angle rearward showed where the oval tube had been cut and rewelded to form the taper. To make the angle, it appeared that the tube had been merely heated with a torch and bent with an iron rod as a fulcrum—this crude but expedient method was chosen by Gilco workers versus the more exacting and careful use of hot sand fillers to aid in bending the tube.

The Superleggera superstructure was formed at Touring of lightweight 20 gauge high-carbon round-section steel tubes. The steel was so malleable, it had probably been bent to shape over a Touring worker's knee. The tubes were welded to the chassis with smooth, even welds, using a gas torch with a tip bore that was much larger than today's; copying these wide welds is difficult for the restorer.

Overall, the chassis was relatively flimsy, and a substantial firewall was used to add stiffness to the racer. The firewall was made of two pieces of C box-section steel, with one piece welded inside of the other for further strength.

The bodywork was composed of handpounded aluminum panels that were unbelievably light. A front fender running from the grille to the door weighed approximately 10 lb. The complete body tipped the scale at about 150 lb, and the chassis and superstructure weighed some 250 lb.

Body panels such as doors and hoods were reinforced at the edges with light-gauge welding rods, around which the aluminum was folded to provide form. Box-section aluminum framework was also added to the inside of the doors and hoods for strength. The frames were fastened to the panels with an extensive array of rivets—approximately one rivet per centimeter running in confused, haphazard lines, which were smoothed over before the body was painted.

Panels were connected to the superstructure with rivets, metal screws, nuts and bolts, and sometimes weld. On structural panels within the car, nuts were often tack-welded in place to be connected to bolts. The long hood vent had been riveted in place with the rivet heads smoothed flat and covered with body filler. At the point where the panels formed the cockpit, the aluminum had been simply rolled over the top steel tube with no fasteners in evidence. Thin strips of leather had been placed between the aluminum body and the steel tubing to curb metal-to-metal corrosion.

The bodywork had been smoothed on an anvil or planishing table, burnished with a hand file and then coated with a type of body-filler-cum-primer made of talc and resin. This talc and resin mix was the norm for early Ferraris. It was sprayed on and left to dry to its matte white color before a true primer and top coats of paint were applied. The filler was surprisingly resilient, holding its own against the elements in this case for forty years.

250 GTO competition *berlinetta* 3223 GT

In the series of thirty-nine 250 GTO competition *berlinette*, the prototype serial number 3223 GT will always be somewhat of an anomaly. It was built in 1962 and constructed almost completely within the walls of Maranello; all other GTOs were built at Scaglietti and Maranello in 1962–64. Thus, even though each 250 GTO differed from the next in minute and large details, 3223 GT was without a doubt unique.

The car began its long history with Scuderia Ferrari before being sold in June 1962 to Luigi Chinetti and imported to the United States to race under the NART banner. It was campaigned at Daytona, Sebring, Nassau and numerous other venues. Over the years, it was brought up to "normal" 250 GTO body configuration with the addition of a full rear spoiler, side marker lights and so on, and many body panels were also refabricated. As of 1990, the car was owned by Bob Bodin of Minneapolis, Minnesota.

As with the Tipo 166 MM, the Testa Rossa Tipo 168 V–12 engine was radical for its time, while the GTO chassis was old-fashioned. Again, the chassis was simple and straightforward: a sturdy, solid and roadworthy piece of work, and nothing more. It was a ladder space frame with oval-section steel tubes braced by an X-member in the center. Zigzag bracing ran beneath the doors with tube outriggers to support the bodywork, as in the Touring concept. Beyond some ad-

Ferrari factory, Maranello, 1962
This famous publicity photograph showed 250 GTO serial number 3223 GT upon its introduction to the press. As with many such press conferences in the early days, this one was held in the factory courtyard. *Robert Bodin Collection*

vances in support and rigidity, the chassis design was inherently similar to that of the Tipo 166 MM.

The aluminum bodywork on the first GTO was handpounded in the race shop by a Scaglietti panelbeater named Agnani, who made the trip from Modena to help. All in all, the panel work was substantially cruder than that of most Ferraris. Engineer Giotto Bizzarrini recalled that not one line of the car was ever drawn on paper; the bodywork was laid out purely by eye. The finished aluminum panels were then joined by sheet metal screws, and the patchwork body was nicknamed Il monstro, or The Monster. After the first race test, the car was renamed La papera, or The Gosling—presumably for its beaklike aerodynamic nose.

An interesting point in the make-up of body panels arises here. Examining a front fender from Tipo 166 MM 0054 M, it's apparent that the single fender was made of at least five separate pieces of aluminum, each handpounded and all then butt-welded together. On 250 GTO 3223 GT, the fabricators used only three or four larger sheets of aluminum similarly connected to form the whole front nose and both fenders. Perhaps the construction style of the Tipo 166 bodywork was due to postwar material shortages and the unavailability of good stock, and thus numerous smaller sheets had to be used to make a single panel.

Detail pieces were added to the front end of the 250 GTO to form the headlight bezels, side marker light pods, characteristic nose vents, side air vents and so on. For the various light bezels, circular aluminum tubing was cut to shape and welded or even riveted into place. The vents were formed from sheet, with the holes simply creased back and folded, and again welded or riveted in. The hood bulge was formed of two aluminum halves that were welded together down a center seam and then mounted with the ubiquitous pop rivets. Thus while the main pieces of the nose and fenders relied on only three to four larger sheets, with all extraneous vents and lights the nose was made up of twenty to twenty-two pieces of metal, including the hood.

Doors and hoods were made of aluminum panels mounted on steel frames, as with the Touring construction of the Tipo 166. A multitude of rivets was again used to attach the panels to the frames. As with the earlier car, a variety of metal screws, nuts and bolts, rivets and weld fastened the panels to the frame. Again, there was little concern for corrosion between steel and aluminum.

Body panels on the 250 GTO ranged between 0.8 and 1.25 mm, or 0.032 and 0.5 in., in thickness—and were thus substantially lighter in gauge than the approximately 2 mm, or 0.08 in., thick panels on the Tipo 166 MM. The complete GTO bodywork weighed 150 to 200 lb.

Carrozzeria Pinin Farina, Grugliasco, 1958
A posed publicity shot within the *carrozzeria* detailed the extent of the design studios; compare this picture with period photographs within Scaglietti! The wooden buck was a model for the Ferrari 410 Superamerica that was to make its debut at the 1958 Paris Salon. The amount of work that went into preparing such mockups to shape body panels on must have been extensive. In the back, a third designer was working a drafting arm on a life-sized sketch of a 250 GT Pinin Farina Coupe. *Pinin Farina, courtesy Automobile Quarterly*

Wallach observed: "A group of fourteen-year-old kids were against one wall pounding out aluminum panels with hammers using tree trunks as molds. There were three styles of tree trunks with concave, convex and flat surfaces for the different panels. In the center, there was a wire form for the body—a *maquette,* as sculptors call it—made up of welding rods welded into the shape of the car. The workers would present the body piece onto the *maquette* to see if it fit, and go back for more shaping if it didn't. Once it fit the form, they handed it to the maestro panelbeater who had a planishing table made of solid steel, two inches thick. He would take a couple swipes at the panel and, *voilà,* beautiful, smooth panels."

Bodywork design

Where the designs for the individual bodywork originated is more ambiguous. Larger *carrozzerie* such as Pinin Farina at Corso Trapani, 107 in Turin had a design staff as developed as their panelbeaters. Working at designboards and drafting altitude sketches—and clay and wood models later on—they would draw and model each design before it was set in metal; the result was a planned, cohesive design. The designs were then translated into the jigs or molds onto which the panels were crafted, and sometimes a single full-scale prototype would be built as a model for the panelbeaters. The smaller shops worked on a smaller scale.

Carrozzeria Pinin Farina, Grugliasco, 1959
While Scaglietti was still forming bodies on tree stumps with welding rod mockups, Pinin Farina had templates with removable forms to measure fit. The wheel templates here were used to ascertain the correct curve for the arch; similar templates were used for other body panels. The panels on this 250 GT had probably been power hammered, as the finish was smooth, lacking the dimples even well-burnished handwork left. Note the hole in the rear fender behind the wheel and the other one used by a worker to aid in welding the steel bodywork to the steel chassis. As of 1958, Pinin Farina construction was close to mass production in working techniques. *Pinin Farina, courtesy Automobile Quarterly*

Pininfarina, Grugliasco, 1966
The paint booth with a line of 330 GT 2+2 bodies after being sprayed with primer. The bodies were again perched on wheeled jigs and were pushed by hand through the stages in the painting process. Lines of heat lights helped bake the paint onto the steel. *Pininfarina, courtesy Automobile Quarterly*

Carrozzeria Fantuzzi, Modena, 1978
The sole hint that this photograph was not taken in the mid 1950s was the antique club automobile registration plate on the Alfa Romeo parked in the rear. Beyond that, the shop and its work techniques were a step back in time. A body was being built for the 1959 model 250 TR, serial number 2030/62E, on the stands at center. In the background at far right rested metal-forming stands of different contours. *Peter Coltrin, courtesy Hilary A. Raab, Jr.*

Carrozzeria Fantuzzi, Modena, 1978
In this further view of the 250 TR, a section of the bodywork being constructed rested against the side wall. The tube-frame superstructure continued Carrozzeria Touring's Superleggera construction heritage. It was connected to the ladder frame at only a few points, allowing the lightweight, easily flexed aluminum bodywork to remain relatively unstressed. *Peter Coltrin, courtesy Hilary A. Raab, Jr.*

In *Ferrari "Le Granturismo,"* French writer Antoine Prunet described how designer Giovanni Michelotti laid out a body shape design on a scale of 1:1 for Alfredo Vignale's coachbuilding shop in Turin, where it was traced directly onto the aluminum sheets that would become the actual body panels. Copying Michelotti's design onto sheet metal was easy; forming the flat metal into flowing curves to match the design relied on artisanship—and a certain amount of imagination. No molds or jigs were used. The panels were first formed with a wooden mallet and the ever-present tree stumps, then refined with a flat hammer and a sandbag, until finally an iron anvil was used for smoothing. Long slender hand files were used to remove blemishes and level the surface. Such techniques worked well when production runs for a single car series numbered only thirteen, as with the Tipo 166 MM Series I and II cars that Vignale clothed.

Even with molds or jigs, body panels were not always identical from car to car within a series—or even from side to side of a single car. Slight differences in compound curves could create contours with different definitions, and the result would be a front end that was asymmetrical in subtle proportions. Prunet quoted Michelotti's colorful explanation: "Just as two human heads are never identical, so a single head is never completely symmetrical." Thus, while the right-hand door may have been larger than the left-hand door or the side windows formed to different shapes, it mattered little. You could see only one side of the car at a time.

Even though Giovanni Michelotti may have penned a design for the 166 Inter, it was up to panelbeaters at Vignale to translate the lines from pen and ink to compound curves of aluminum, and with that translation came a certain amount of poetic license. Likewise, Pinin Farina's designs were often subcontracted out and put into metal by workers at Scaglietti and Boano, and Pinin Farina's theoretical design on paper or its prototype jig may have needed alterations to become a practical automobile in aluminum or steel; it was up to the panelbeater to make it all fit. The photographs from *Road & Track*'s visit to Scaglietti in 1956 illustrate this. In one picture a worker fits to the 860 Monza's hood a single low pan that was to account for the tall stance of the 3.5 liter inline four-cylinder engine. The single hood bulge does not clear the twin cam covers—or perhaps does not please aesthetically. In the next photo, a second worker is eyeing the appeal of two elongated canoe-shaped hood bulges that follow the cam covers while also echoing the lines of the fenders. In the end, neither design was used on the six cars built.

The panelbeating technique also answered the question of cost for a fledgling factory like Ferrari. When production runs were low, the accountants' quantities of scale forbade the making of molds for a mechanized bodywork press to stamp out panels, as were being used by mass-production auto makers such as Mercedes-Benz. These costs would have been impossible for Ferrari—and Enzo Ferrari may have chosen against such mass production even if it had been available to him, as the handwork allowed for custom bodies and flexibility in making changes to designs.

This ease of modification and design inherent in panelbeating suited Enzo Ferrari to perfection. Each car was unique, each car was a special—even when produced in what Ferrari at the time considered a model series. As Ferrari stated in his memoirs, "I should like to put

Carrozzeria Fantuzzi, Modena, circa 1985
Little had changed—including the cars being worked on. Against the far wall
rested several Ferrari sports racers and a short-wheelbase 250 GT Scaglietti
Berlinetta. The car being restored was a mid 1950s Mille Miglia racer. Note
the English wheel at rear—a rare sight in an Italian *carrozzeria! Hilary A.
Raab, Jr.*

Carrozzeria Fantuzzi, Modena, circa 1985
Planishing tables, hand files and hammers were the tools used to reconstruct
the aluminum bodywork of the Mille Miglia car. Note the drilled-out frame
structure for the doors. *Hilary A. Raab, Jr.*

Carrozzeria Scaglietti, Modena, circa 1975
The wooden buck for forming the front end of the 275 GTB/4 was still in use behind the Scaglietti workshop. A finished metal section waited to be lifted off; underneath, the framework of the buck was visible, offering a rare look at how such bucks were constructed. Based on a square-section metal stand, the wooden forms were hung at working height. The metal body panel sheets were tested for fit on the buck during the handpounding of the panels. *Hilary A. Raab, Jr.*

Carrozzeria Scaglietti, Modena, 1976
Tools of the old ways were still in everyday use. A worker fabricated headlamp carriers for a 365 GT4 BB at a worktable. Behind him stood wooden bucks for forming the BB doors. A steel planishing table, a rounded forming stand and an anvil waited in the shop. Stacked against the rear wall were rear fenders for 246 GT Dinos, some two years after the last model was produced. *Hilary A. Raab, Jr.*

something new into my cars every morning.... Were my wishes in this respect to be indulged, there would be no production of standard models at all, but only a succession of prototypes." Until the 250 GT series, which made its debut in 1956, Ferrari's wish came true—every morning. Thus, the uniformity of a model series such as the luxurious road-going 250 GT SWB Spyder California was determined far more by product identity than by production standards, while the uniformity of the thirty-nine examples of the racing 250 GTO was set more by homologation requirements.

Customers also had a say in the silhouette their car would wear. In an interview with Angelo Tito Anselmi in *Ferrari Tipo 166*, Carlo Felice Bianchi Anderloni, director of Carrozzeria Touring, told of the steps involved in overseeing a custom-bodied Tipo 166: "All Ferrari's customers came into contact with Touring sooner or later. The routine procedure was simple enough: Ferrari ordered the bodywork here and dispatched the chassis to us. While the work was being carried out he sold the car. Invariably the client would come here to see the car in the various stages of its construction, asking for particular personal touches, choosing the colours, taking possession of their 'little toy' before it was finished, becoming friends with the men who were building it."

Steel stampings

By the 1970s, much had changed at coachbuilders such as Scaglietti and Pininfarina (previously Pinin Farina). A series of photographs taken by Peter Coltrin captured the Scaglietti coachbuilders at work finishing and fitting body panels to 246 GT Dino chassis, with a line of 365 GTB/4 Daytonas alongside. A single line of Dino chassis ran the length of the expanded Modena shop, with the cars set on wheeled dollies and the wheels on one side of those dollies rolling down a simple metal track for ease of movement—still a giant's step from an assembly line. Although the number of cars being constructed at one time had changed little from the dozen in 1958, something was absent from the Dino line. No tree trunks, sandbags, planishing tables or anvils were at hand.

Sometime in 1969, during the run of the 246 GT series, production was changed from hand-beaten to machine-stamped body panels. To be sure, early versions of the model appeared with hand-beaten bodies, as it required time to ready tooling. But beginning with the Dino, Ferrari was finally producing enough cars to justify the costs of tooling dies for pressure-stamping of body panels. Financing for this venture was a large step, a result of the 1969 influx of capital into Ferrari from Fiat's partial purchase and the Turinese firm's subsequent acquisition of Scaglietti in 1970–71. With the arrival of the Porsche 911, Ferrari—and Fiat—was spurred to expand. And with large-scale production of body panels for the Dino, back rooms at Scaglietti suddenly were stocked for storing row upon row of rough pressed bodywork that arrived from Pininfarina; the old coachbuilding wire molds were cast out.

Even though everything had changed at Scaglietti and Pininfarina in terms of body building for the 246 GT, everything remained the same in the finishing and fitting of the panels. The Coltrin photographs show the large workforce employed by Scaglietti for the labor-intensive tasks; some ten workers attend to three or four Dino bodies

Carrozzeria Scaglietti, Modena, 1969
Bodywork construction for the 246 GT and the 365 GTB/4 within the expanded *carrozzeria* works. The tree stumps and planishing tables were things of the past; body panels for the Dino were now fabricated at the large Pininfarina factory and trucked to Scaglietti for assembly. Dino panels were set into dies and machine-stamped, a process possible owing to the large production runs. Daytona panels were formed with power hammers, electric machines shaped like an English wheel but using a mechanical hammer on the top to pound the metal over dollies. The panels were then hammer-welded, planished and burnished by hand. *Peter Coltrin, courtesy Hilary A. Raab, Jr.*

Carrozzeria Scaglietti, Modena, 1969
At center, a worker finished the shaping of a 365 GTB/4 hood with a flat-faced metalworking hammer. At right, another worker smoothed the metal surface of a trunk lid with an electric belt sander. Some of the tools had changed, but the job was still much the same and labor-intensive. The body of the Daytona rested atop a wheeled jig that was pushed by hand down a track; the first stage to an actual assembly line. *Peter Coltrin, courtesy Hilary A. Raab, Jr.*

Carrozzeria Scaglietti, Modena, 1969
In the old days, welding rod molds for body panels were stacked against walls in the *carrozzeria's* sole workroom. With the new shop and the expanded production, the wire molds were cast out and storerooms were built. Here, 365 GTB/4 noses with the tails nestled inside sat at left with body panels for the 246 GT at right. These panels were fresh from Pininfarina, awaiting assembly. *Peter Coltrin, courtesy Hilary A. Raab, Jr.*

Carrozzeria Scaglietti, Modena, 1975
Out with the old, in with the new: the junk area outdoors behind the coachbuilding works. With the increase in production and the use of more modern methods, Scaglietti had cleaned out its old equipment to make room for storing machine-pressed body panels arriving from Pininfarina. Several Ferrari sports racer body forms made of iron welding rods rusted against the wall, packed in with discarded nose sections to other Ferraris, including the 275 GTB/4. A sad sight. *Hilary A. Raab, Jr.*

in one picture. Finishing work included minor planishing with flat-faced metalworking hammers and honing of the metal surfaces with electric belt sanders. Other workers used sandpaper held in hand to touch up rough edges on hoods and hand-fit the panels to the chassis. The creasing of edges and smoothing of seams was all handwork.

The mating of the bodywork to the chassis also took a further step with the 246 GT. In the early days, Ferrari had sent out to the *carrozzerie* rolling chassis complete with engines and all mechanicals in working order; the coachbuilders built the bodies in their shops and welded them to the chassis. With the erection of the assembly lines at Maranello during the 250 GT series, the body and chassis were constructed independent of the mechanicals at Scaglietti and Pinin Farina. The completed body-chassis combination was then transferred by truck to Maranello where the engine was dropped in place and the entire driveline and interior were added; electrics were done either at Ferrari or at the coachbuilder, depending on the car model.

The result of this change in progression of assembly steps can be seen on the 250 GT series cars. In the days when the chassis was assembled at Maranello and delivered to the coachbuilder for covering, a steel rod was run from the engine to the top of the freestanding radiator to support the radiator in place. This rod showed up on the Tour de France cars, the 250 Europas, the first series 250 GT Cabriolets and several other series. When the production lines were erected at Maranello sometime in 1958–60, the chassis and body were already mated by the time Ferrari assemblers began work. The radiators could now be secured more firmly, using a mount much like an exhaust hanger to fasten them directly to the bodywork. This mounting style appears to have started with the 250 GT Pinin Farina Coupe.

By 1970, Ferrari had consolidated most of its work within the family of Scaglietti and Pininfarina. The chassis framework was built by Vaccari on the northern side of Modena. Next the chassis was transferred across the city to Scaglietti, which constructed the body and painted it, and then moved the chassis-body on a rolling jig to a finishing room where the electrics were fitted. From there the cars were trailered to Maranello where interiors were appointed, the engine was dropped in, the driveline was connected and the car was finished. This process continued until the mid 1970s, when the upholstery shop was shifted to Ferrari beginning with the 308 GTB and when, in 1978, the large paint shop was erected at Maranello and bare bodies were shipped from Scaglietti to the factory.

Nevertheless, while Scaglietti and Pininfarina shifted to pressure-stamping of body panels in 1969, the rule was broken on the neighboring line of 365 GTB/4 Daytonas, which were still constructed with hand-beaten and power-hammered panels. The panels were formed at Pininfarina and trucked to Scaglietti. For fitting and finishing the Daytonas at Scaglietti, large jigs were used with hinged exterior molds that could be swung away from the body for ease of work.

The move to using pressed bodywork was again bypassed in 1971 with the introduction of the 365 GT4 BB. Ferrari planned to build the Berlinetta Boxer as a limited-run road racer; however, customer demand eventually drove the series into ongoing production through the 512 BBi, discontinued in 1984. Based on initial planning for the car, the bodies were handmade at Scaglietti, even in the early 1980s when 512 BBi annual production reached 200 to 250 cars. Thus, as of 1990, the Berlinetta Boxers—and the 275 GTB/4 and 365 GTB/4 before them—were the last Ferraris with hand-beaten coachwork.

Le carrozzerie in 1990

Visiting the remaining *carrozzerie* in 1989 was a lesson in contrasts. Several venerable coachbuilders continued business into the 1990s. Bertone, which performed limited work for Ferrari through the years, had made its reputation with Lamborghini, Alfa Romeo and others. Zagato maintained its low-volume work for clients such as Aston Martin and Alfa Romeo. Others, such as Carrozzeria Fantuzzi, lived on in much the same vein as when the coachbuilder first bodied Ferraris in the 1950s.

The Fantuzzi works on the edge of Modena looked like a time machine in 1989, owing to the working techniques and the cars being worked on—restoration of vintage Ferraris, from a 340 America to a 250 GT SWB. Panels were made from aluminum and steel both by panelbeating and with the aid of an English wheel, a rare machine in the shop of an Italian coachbuilder. Steel planishing tables and an array of metalworker hammers and files hung squarely by hooks on the walls. Panels were fitted to the tube chassis much as before, with the time-consuming work of adjusting them to fit by hand. Acetylene and oxygen tanks awaited the final welding, the hoses neatly coiled out of the way. The only new sound was that of electric disc sanders. Modern lighted plastic Ferrari signs marked the entranceway.

Scaglietti and Pininfarina had gone on to supply Ferrari with its cars' silhouettes. As of 1989, Scaglietti was building the composite

Carrozzeria Scaglietti, Modena, 1969
In the finishing room at the *carrozzeria,* cars were in all different stages of production, from the freshly painted 246 GT at center, to the other Dino at right, complete with trim, bumpers, glass, and wheels and tires. In the foreground at left was a 365 GTB/4 halfway through assembly, with weather stripping and trim recently added. The room visible in the back appeared to contain more cars awaiting finishing work. *Peter Coltrin, courtesy Hilary A. Raab, Jr.*

Carrozzeria Scaglietti, Modena, 1979
Two chassis waited for the assembly line on a trailer after being delivered from the Vaccari frame works on the other side of Modena. This means of storing chassis was one reason for the prevalent rust on many 250 GT series Ferraris—the rust got an early start on the chassis after they had sat out in one-too-many Emilian rainstorms. *Hilary A. Raab, Jr.*

Vaccari, Modena, 1978
Through the years, the strength of Ferrari chassis largely relied on the inherent structural strength of oval tubing versus heavier-gauge round tubing. Here was the store of oval-section tubing destined for Ferrari chassis, waiting behind the Vaccari frame-making works in Modena. *Hilary A. Raab, Jr.*

Carrozzeria Scaglietti, Modena, circa 1977
With the 512 BB replacing the 365 GT4 BB, the old wooden buck for forming the first Berlinetta Boxer bodies was discarded among piles of wooden pallets at Scaglietti, to make way for a new mockup to form the panels for the new car. A fiberglass nose section for an unidentified sports racer rested on top of the buck. *Hilary A. Raab, Jr.*

Carrozzeria Scaglietti, Modena, 1975
While body panels for the 308 GT4 and 365 GT4 2+2 were being machine-stamped at Pininfarina, Scaglietti was making bodies for the 365 GT4 BB by hand, with the aid of power hammers. Initial production for the Berlinetta Boxer was planned to be low, so tooling was not made for machine pressing of panels. Here, a group of bare BB bodies was being assembled at Scaglietti; the line bore more than a passing resemblance to the Daytona line of some six years earlier. *Hilary A. Raab, Jr.*

bodywork and steel tube chassis for the F40, and the steel bodywork for the V–8 engined production cars from the 308 GTB series and Mondial to the first 348 tb and 348 ts of 1990. Pininfarina was building the bodywork for the Testarossa and assembling much of the car in Grugliasco, with the chassis subcontracted out. The two companies had grown up well with Ferrari.

Pininfarina and the Testarossa

Giovanni Battista "Pinin" Farina was the grand old coachbuilder of Ferraris—Enzo Ferrari's friend and the man who gave personality to Ferrari's automobiles. Over the years, Carrozzeria Pininfarina designed and bodied more Ferrari models than did the other coachbuilders combined.

Pininfarina always stood out from the other *carrozzerie* in work technique as well. The smaller coachbuilders such as Zagato and Fantuzzi built one-off bodies by hand; even in 1990, these shops continued with the same mode of construction. Pininfarina grew with the times and the techniques, keeping pace with Ferrari's increasing demand for bodywork through the years from the early Tipo 212 Inters to the expansion with the 250 GT series. Only Scaglietti—which often subcontracted work from Pininfarina—followed in Pininfarina's footsteps.

The quality of work performed at Pininfarina always stood out from that of the other coachbuilders, even with mass production in the 1980s. Scaglietti's work bore the imprint of a handbuilt body, while Pininfarina's quality showed through in the complexity of designs, the beauty of weld beads, panel forming, uniformity of seams and so on. Pininfarina's quality of work was largely reserved for the road cars, while Drogo, Fantuzzi and others clothed the racers.

Until 1952, when Carrozzeria Pinin Farina designed and bodied its first Tipo 212 Inter, Ferrari had courted numerous coachbuilders, yet had not entered into a long-term partnership with any of them. On one hand, Ferrari was unable and unwilling to build sufficient production runs of cars with any uniformity, making it impossible for a single coachbuilder to contribute more than a design here and there. On the other hand, Ferrari was guarded about entering into such a marriage with another constructor and sharing the fame. Ferrari wanted his cars to bear only the prancing horse emblem, the *cavallino rampante*.

Ferrari's willingness to join hands with Pinin Farina in 1952 must have played on two key issues: the prestige of the *carrozzeria* as the finest coachbuilder of *granturismo* cars; and Enzo Ferrari's friendship and trust of Battista Farina. Only such conditions would have suited Ferrari.

Early on, Pinin Farina demonstrated its ability as being above and beyond the competing coachbuilders. While others were eyeballing designs and fitting panels to mockups built of welding rods, Pinin Farina was in the avant-garde. As early as the mid 1950s, Pinin Farina designers used floor-to-ceiling drawing boards to draft actual-size altitude sketches. Scale clay models were formed, and wooden bucks were built to craft the prototype panels around. Such expertise and artistry was out of the realm of Scaglietti and most of the others.

As early as 1958, Pinin Farina was set up in its new expanded works in the Turinese suburb of Grugliasco and producing 250 GT coupe chassis and bodies on a scale that was perhaps ahead of even

Carrozzeria Scaglietti, Modena, 1975
The paint booth at Scaglietti. With bake lights overhead, a line of 308 GT4 bodies passed down the track to be hand-sprayed. The workers had no protection from the paint fumes or spray. In 1978, a new paint shop was erected at Maranello, and all Scaglietti-bodied Ferraris were painted there. *Hilary A. Raab, Jr.*

Maranello's. Mechanized, hand-held spot welders were used to form bodywork, and chassis were rolled down a style of production line atop wheeled jigs. In pictures of the era, a team of three workers surround the car, each attacking different segments in a style akin to American assembly line practices.

By the mid 1960s, the coachbuilder had further refined its construction, and the designs and bodies of most series-production Ferraris began life at Pinin Farina. Along with its continuing success, the coachbuilder changed its name to Pininfarina in 1961. In 1969, the *carrozzeria* led the way with Ferrari in machine-stamping body panels for the Dino 246 GT.

Pininfarina was also the first *carrozzeria* to build a wind tunnel for aerodynamic analysis of automobile body designs, in 1972. Moto Guzzi built one of Italy's first *galleria del vento* at Mandello del Lario in 1950, and several universities had early wind tunnels of their own by the 1960s. In developing the 250 GTO, Ferrari engineer Giotto Bizzarrini was forced to travel to the University of Pisa's wind tunnel to test the revolutionary aerodynamic bodywork; further fine-tuning was done on the racetrack with the aid of driver Richie Ginther, in the best Ferrari tradition. Before building its wind tunnel, Pininfarina used the one at the Turin Polytechnic Institute to mirror-model test the first 250 LM.

In the 1980s, Ferrari coachbuilding was weighted toward Scaglietti in terms of volume with the 308 GTB series, but Pininfarina produced Ferrari's flagship model, the Testarossa, relying on the Turinese company's quality of design and detail work. During the production run of the Testarossa, Pininfarina delivered the completed and painted body-chassis assemblies to Maranello. At this stage, the

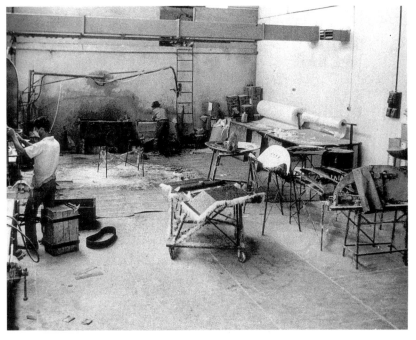

Carrozzeria Scaglietti, Modena, 1969
The first use of fiberglass in Ferraris came with the Dino and Daytona; here was Scaglietti's fiberglass shop in full swing. Molds were used, set atop jigs, and fiberglass cloth was unrolled and cut to shape. The cloth was laid into the molds and coated with resin in alternating layers. The worker at left appeared to be trimming fiberglass panels. Scrap glass fibers covered the floor and jig stands. *Peter Coltrin, courtesy Hilary A. Raab, Jr.*

Carrozzeria Scaglietti, Modena, 1976
Fresh from the fiberglass room, a group of first-series 308 GTB bodies sat amid the steel 308 GT4s. The fiberglass was designed by Pininfarina and was laid at Scaglietti in the downtime while tooling was prepared to machine stamp the steel body panels intended for the regular-production 308 GTB. As of 1990, these first-series 308 GTBs were the only cars Ferrari built wearing fiberglass bodies. *Hilary A. Raab, Jr.*

electrics and lights of the cars were all in working order. Interiors, drivetrains and engines were added at Ferrari.

Pininfarina's factory in the 1980s was a large nondescript industrial works in Grugliasco covering 151,000 square meters, or 1,625,000 square feet, with 81,000 square meters, or 871,000 square feet, occupied by the factory buildings. In the nearby town of Cambiano, Pininfarina's *studi e ricerche* center provided research and development for the company. The coachbuilder now owned by Fiat also built bodies for Fiat and others, such as the Cadillac Allante, and even marketed its own factory-built car, the Pininfarina Spider, based on the Fiat 124 Spider. As of 1989, the factory employed 2,000 workers—thirty-six percent more workers than were at Maranello, eighty-nine percent more than were at Scaglietti.

Scaglietti in the 1990s: Robotics and composites

The headquarters offices for the new Ferrari Engineering were housed alongside the Scaglietti shop at via Emilia Est, 1103, with the actual coachbuilding works set back from the old main Modena-Bologna road, just down the street from the Ferrari concessionaire. Scaglietti had moved to the via Emilia Est, 1103 shop in 1959. The parking lot of the *carrozzeria* in 1989 was filled with an untidy clutter of boxy Fiats, rickety mopeds and squat Vespas, a stark contrast to the cars made within the Modena-yellow walls of Scaglietti.

Inside, the factory wing where the bodies for the V-8 production cars were built was far more modernized than were the Maranello works. Monstrous futuristic welding robots and smaller manned spot-welding machines moved around Ferrari chassis clamped into a latticework of jigs like patients trussed up in traction. Cascades of yellow sparks showered from the machines in blasts of fireworks.

Off to the sides of the main production lines, workers tended to the details with hand tools—powered both by electricity and by muscle—taking time to smooth the edges on retractable headlamp covers for an early 348, held in place by a worktable vise. Other workers used electric sanders to finish door panels, checking the fit, and triggering the sander again. Much of the work was done by robotics and manned welders, but the finer work was all performed by hand. In a special booth, workers in protective clothing checked and smoothed the bodywork built by the machines.

In the mid 1970s, Ferraris shared the work space with bulky industrial cabs built for Fiat tractors, which made up a percentage of Scaglietti's work. The tractor production came out of union demands to parent company Fiat: with the toll the oil crisis was taking on the exotic car market and the jobs it supported, the unions wished to diversify their job dependence. Scaglietti thus picked up the Fiat tractor work. The paint booth and interior trim shop for Ferraris were soon moved to Maranello.

By 1989, Fiat tractor production had transferred on to specialized plants, and construction of the composite bodywork, chassis and many components for the limited-run F40 had been set up. Centered in two medium-sized rooms across a central alley from the V-8 car wing, the work on the F40 was a revival of the labor-intensive level of the late 1960s—albeit with materials of the 1990s. In one corner, a chassis was being built with formed sheets and tubes of OP 10 steel locked together in a large cagelike jig. One chassis was fabricated at a time. A single

Carrozzeria Scaglietti, Modena, 1976
The early fiberglass-bodied 308 GTBs were finished on the line at Scaglietti.
The bodies were set atop wheeled jigs and run down the line much as the
steel-and-alloy-bodied Ferraris before them; in the background was the line
for the 365 GT4 2+2. The fiberglass 308 GTBs were constructed as transi-
tional cars before the steel panels could be cut into dies. About 1,200 fiberglass
308 GTBs were built with 200 US versions. *Hilary A. Raab, Jr.*

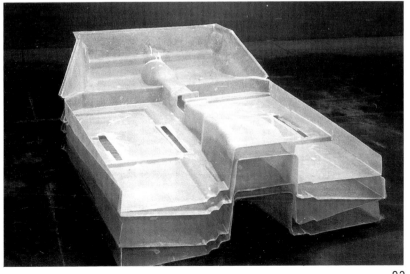

Pininfarina, Grugliasco, 1977
Neat stack of finished fiberglass floor pans for 400 GTs. In the old days,
dozens of separate metal sheets would have been cut to size and shape, formed
and then butt-welded or riveted together to form such an underbody section.
With fiberglass, a single mold could be used with glass laid and resin coated in
little time. *Hilary A. Raab, Jr.*

Carrozzeria Scaglietti, Modena, 1989
The steel chassis destined for a V–8 production car was dwarfed within a mechanical jig for forming the chassis. Set up within the jig, the chassis was spot-welded together complete with templates used to ensure the final fit. From here the chassis would be mated with the exterior bodywork and welded together by the robots.

worker bent over the frame with a welding torch, hand-welding the frame together piece by piece, the solitary flame of the torch reflected in the welding mask. From there, the frame was set onto a stand and two workers hovered over it with glue guns, squirting long snakes of adhesives along the frame and attaching the other chassis components: door strut covers, floor panels and a front bulkhead all constructed of a Nomex and Kevlar-carbon-fiber weave; rear and side panels made of honeycomb aluminum.

The composite body panels for the F40 were molded in an autoclave (a large, tunnellike steam oven) by a subcontractor and delivered

Carrozzeria Scaglietti, Modena, 1989
While the mechanized welders ran through their programs in the background, a worker fabricated a Ferrari hood by hand with the aid of a welding torch. The disparity between robotics and labor-intensive handwork was everywhere on the line at the *carrozzeria*.

Carrozzeria Scaglietti, Modena, 1989
A worker finished the lip of a pop-up headlamp section with the aid of an electric sander. Much of the labor at Scaglietti was done by automated machines, but detail work was still by hand.

Carrozzeria Scaglietti, Modena, 1989
Body panels for V–8 production cars were machined-stamped, producing uniform steel. Burnishing of the stamp's bodywork was all done by hand, however, with the help of an electric disc sander. Special high-intensity fluorescent lights within the finishing booth allowed workers to spot any impurities in the steel panels.

Carrozzeria Scaglietti, Modena, 1989
Mechanized spot welders were manned to fabricate steel chassis for V–8 production cars. Note the use of clamps as in the old days. The quality of worker protection had also changed little.

to the Scaglietti plant. When the F40 bodywork was first added to the chassis, hours were spent with the same long slender hand file used years ago to burnish the hand-beaten metal. A sole worker, cloaked in a floor-length white apron coated in composite tailings, ran the file over curves and flats, checking the smoothness with his hand, bending down to look at it from different angles and against the overhead lights, until he was satisfied with the finish. Without their later coats of pink primer and red paint, the composite bodies were pale and anemic looking, a ghostly white. From the Scaglietti workshop, the F40s were rolled out into the sun and loaded onto a Fiat truck, bound for Maranello.

Ferrari reported that the tooling of molds for the steam-heated presses and vacuums for the composite components and bodywork was much less expensive than were the dies for pressed-metal body panels, making such limited production *almost* economical. This use of adhesives and composite materials was a revolution in Ferrari road car construction and an evolution from Formula One car construction— continuing the history of Ferrari race and road car development from the Tipo 166 on.

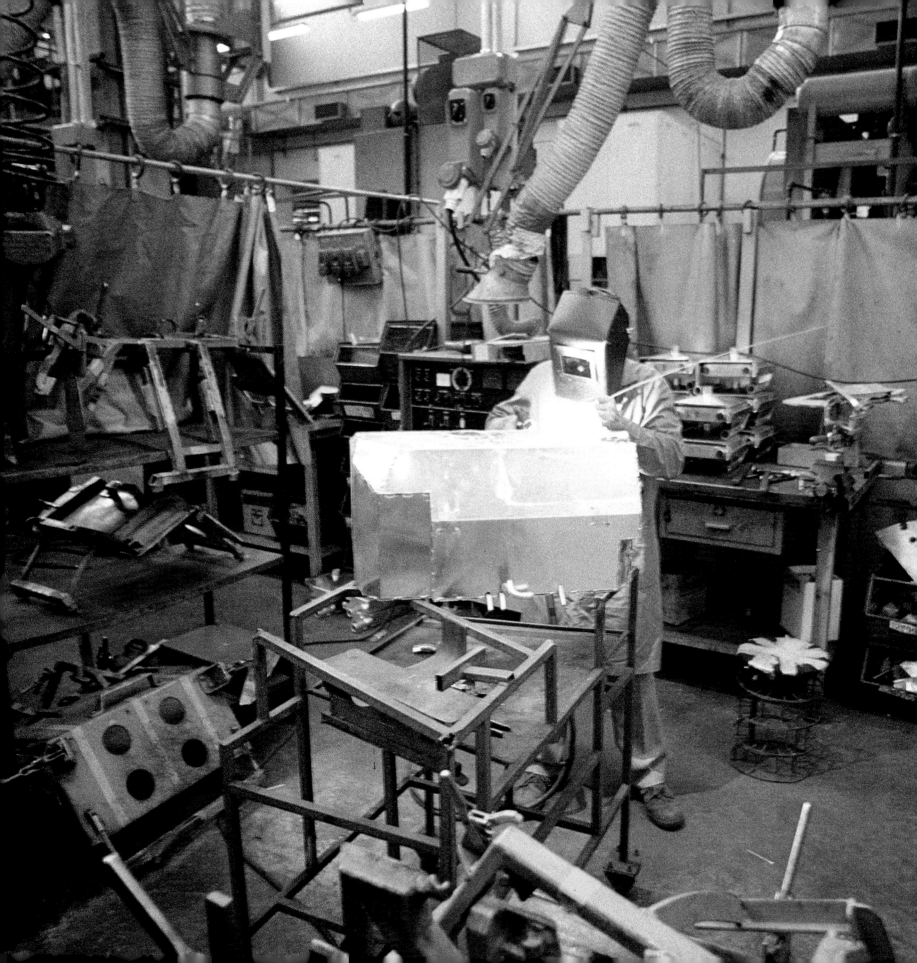

Carrozzeria Scaglietti, Modena, 1989
A simple test for airtightness was performed on F40 gas tanks. Fresh from the welder, the tanks were plugged and then submerged in water to check for leaks. If air bubbles were spotted rising from the tank, it was sent back.

Previous page
Carrozzeria Scaglietti, Modena, 1989
Set off from the body production sectors, mufflers and gas tanks for the F40 were fabricated. Stamping machines cut out the patterns, which were then welded together by hand.

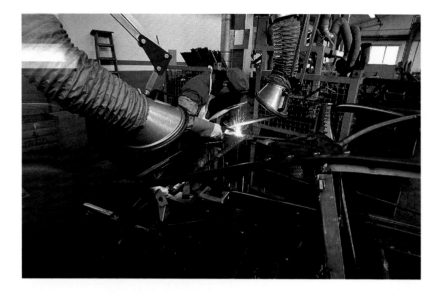

Carrozzeria Scaglietti, Modena, 1989
Another wing of the Scaglietti works was another world in terms of work techniques. Across the alley from the V–8 production car sector, chassis and bodywork for the F40 were fabricated. This area contained no robots, no mechanized equipment beyond welding torches. Here a worker constructed an F40 frame, made of OP 10 steel tubing.

Carrozzeria Scaglietti, Modena, 1989
The lower tail section was added to the F40 chassis. The body panel was made of composite materials, supported on the frame by thin tubing, much as with Carrozzeria Touring's early Superleggera system.

Carrozzeria Scaglietti, Modena, 1989
With the steel tubework frame welded up, a worker added the composite structural supports. Long snakes of adhesive were laid on the tubing, and here the backrest side panels were glued in place. The side panels were made of aluminum and honeycomb. Floor pans and front spare tire carrier were then added, made of Kevlar carbon fiber; the bulkhead and door side panels were fabricated of a Nomex and Kevlar-carbon-fiber weave.

Carrozzeria Scaglietti, Modena, 1989
A primed F40 body waited in the central alleyway between the V–8 production car sector and the small F40 wing. As in the past, the bodies were moved about on wheeled jigs, powered by human muscle. In front of the F40 was a steel-bodied Mondial t Cabriolet.

Carrozzeria Scaglietti, Modena, 1989
Off the main F40 construction sector, the body was finished in another room. Using sandpaper and a hand file, a worker smoothed down the composite material to ready it for priming. The body would then be painted at Maranello.

Chapter 4

The Foundry

Aluminum and Electron Sand Casting

For a factory the size of Ferrari to have its own foundry, metal-plating and heat-treating shops is nothing short of incredible, a testament to Enzo Ferrari's desire to have control over the quality of all components under his hand. Still, the magnitude of this operation for such a small factory is difficult to comprehend, seemingly possible only in the specialized world of Italian car makers. Fiat in Turin was large enough and producing enough cars to support its own mass-production foundry. Alfa Romeo in Milan, while primarily building race cars and exotic grand touring cars for the rich, also had a foundry. Maserati, on the other side of Modena, had its own foundry by the early 1950s, as the company was well established and well financed, having been founded in 1914 and infused with capital in 1937 by Modenese industrialist Omer Orsi.

Ferrari foundry, Maranello, 1989
After the metal had been poured, it was allowed to cool and set before the walls of mold were backed away, leaving the shining block standing free.

Ferrari foundry, Maranello, 1989
Cast crankshaft main bearing caps fresh from the foundry waited to be machined.

Following in the footsteps of Ferrari after World War II, not even Ferruccio Lamborghini at Sant'Agata Bolognese had his own foundry, despite his well-financed beginnings in sports car construction. For Lamborghini's first V–12 engines, the casting work was ordered out—from former Ferrari engineer Carlo Chiti's Automobili Turismo Sport, or ATS, in Modena, the ill-fated sports and Formula One car constructor started by Count Volpi di Misurata and his Scuderia Serenissima at Pontecchio Marconi, near Bologna. Lamborghini later subcontracted to Ferrari's former foundry, Calzoni; who knows what construction secrets were shared. Lamborghini's moving from foundry to foundry in its later years had less to do with work quality complaints than with staying a step ahead of bill collectors and past-due bills, according to Bob Wallace.

Specialist race car builders like Stanguellini, Ermini, Cisitalia, Abarth, Nardi, Siata and the numerous others modified production engines for their own cars and hired foundry work for their special cylinder heads and manifolds. Other constructors such as Alejandro de Tomaso, Carlo Rivolta, Giotto Bizzarrini and the Swiss Peter Monteverdi took a practical route: they ordered proprietary V–8 engines from the United States in finished form.

Ferrari saw a foundry as a necessity. To experiment with the designs the engineers were turning out, a foundry offered flexibility

and ease of construction. Changes could be made from one engine casting to the next at low cost owing to the use of basic sand molds; experimentation was possible with expedience. Alloys could be studied and altered from car to car, and special Electron components could be cast for the race shop. Finally, secrecy of design and engineering could be assured.

Ferrari strove to do as much of its own foundry work as soon as feasible, Wallace remembered: "The foundry was a basic part of the factory, a basic concept of going racing. To race, you have to adapt and modify—and do it all right the first time. And when you look back at the fact that Ferrari has built well over 200 types of engines, they had to have a foundry in the factory."

Early casting work

When Ferrari constructed his first race car in Modena following the split with Alfa Romeo, he chose to build his own engine, although using many parts from the ubiquitous Fiat 508C Balilla. Ferrari designer Alberto Massimino mated two Fiat 1100 cc aluminum cylinder heads together to cap the specially cast engine block, made on contract by the Fonderia Calzoni in Bologna. The hire of casting work came as no surprise: Ferrari was running strictly a race team with none of the resources of an automobile maker at hand.

Ferrari continued to contract Alessandro Calzoni's foundry to cast engine blocks and other aluminum alloy components from sand molds for its first Tipo 125 V–12 engines. The factory worked with Calzoni from 1946 to 1954, in the years before the foundry was erected at Maranello.

Some historians state that casting work was also hired until 1954 from the Maserati foundry in Modena. This seems doubtful. That the two Italian racing arch rivals would cooperate and share facilities would come as a grand surprise, especially in this early period when Ferrari was first mounting his challenge. It's also doubtful that Ferrari would allow Maserati's owner Omer Orsi such intimate contact with the engineering of Ferrari's engines, design secrets that could be priceless to a competitor.

Bob Wallace added a final word to the debate. Never mind questions of racing rivalry, design secrets or technical espionage; the truth was much more simple: politics. "Enzo Ferrari and Signor Orsi did not get on well," Wallace remembered.

Sand castings

Ferrari built its foundry within the walls of the Maranello factory in 1954. During an early visit to the factory, Phil Hill toured the

Ferrari foundry, Maranello, circa 1958
The worker holding the right end of the pot poured molten aluminum alloy into a sand mold while the worker at left pivoted the carrying rod. All the metal was poured into the one sprue; the additional holes served as vents to allow the displaced air an escape route and to let off the steam from the wet sand. The worker at far right was setting up a cylinder head mold, placing pattern pieces into the sand. The metal tray at center held the beginning of an engine block casting; core passages for the cylinders were visible. This was probably a staged publicity photograph showing the stages of the casting work—the workers were wearing protective goggles, but no gloves! *Peter Coltrin Collection, courtesy Hilary A. Raab, Jr.*

foundry just after it had started work. He admired the self-sufficiency of Ferrari's work and the "impressive backyard-style foundry," as he recalled it.

Within the foundry, Ferrari cast engine casings for all his cars, from road to race. Aluminum alloys and Electron magnesium alloys could all be mixed and experimented with to the engineer's metallurgical needs.

Ferrari made castings from sand molds, which were formed to cast aluminum alloy or Electron into large bulky components, such as engine blocks, cylinder heads, transmission cases and so on. Sand casting was used because it offered numerous benefits to a factory of Ferrari's size and assets, and despite its crudeness and limitations. Sand was quick, inexpensive and easy to use, and could be simply modified for any design changes or prototype work. Tooled die-cast molds were

Ferrari foundry, Maranello, circa 1958
All stages of the aluminum alloy casting work were visible in this press release overview of the foundry, erected in 1954. Beginning with the metal trays, the fine black casting sand was sifted in place. Next, patterns were pushed into the sand to form the molds and core passages were added. The worker at right was

pounding sprues and vents into the sand to allow for the molten alloy to be poured in and the steam to be displaced. In the background, the alloy was being poured. On the shelves against the wall rested the vent molds, core passage patterns and some finished castings, cleaned of sand. *Peter Coltrin Collection, courtesy Hilary A. Raab, Jr.*

made up only for components on cars that were to be built in large production runs, such as the V-8 engine block for the 308 GTB series. The techniques of casting components at Ferrari were timeless, mirroring the sculptor's use of sand molds in casting bronze statues or jewelry, a method of artistry dating back to Italian Renaissance masters such as Donatello in the 1400s.

To form a sand mold for casting an engine cylinder head in the Ferrari foundry of the 1950s, the molds were designed from the inside working out. A pattern for the cylinder head was carved of wood—which was not an easy job; it was no surprise that many of the finest woodworkers of the time were pattern makers for foundries. The pattern was made slightly oversize in all dimensions in comparison with the desired, finished casting. This was done for several reasons: first, excess material would be machined away, and second, the aluminum alloy would contract upon cooling.

Two large metal trays were used to hold the sand that the cylinder head would be cast from. These were paired together like the two halves of a clamshell, with locating pins to align them perfectly face to face, making certain the molds would line up.

Two types of sand were used to form the mold. First, a basic coarse-grain sand was packed into the metal trays around the outside; this served to fill the excess space around the form. Next, a special foundry sand was packed in the center to make the mold. This was an extremely fine-grain sand, like baking flour, and was usually blended with water or a resin so it would hold together in all the details of its form.

The wood cylinder head pattern was sawn in half for the two sides of the sand-filled trays. The pattern was forced into the fine-grain sand and then removed, leaving its shape imprinted. This impression would be the outer walls of the final casting.

The forming of the inside oil galleys, valve passages, inlet and exhaust cylinder ports, hemispherical cylinder domes, stud holes and so on was much more difficult. Although a simple wooden positive pattern could be carved for the cylinder head as a whole, the passages had to be made in reverse: the cores of the passages themselves had to be carved as molds—and each bore or galleyway had to be a separate piece. In addition, these molds had to be made from a material that would stand up to the heat of molten metal, as they would remain in the sand casting during the pouring. Thus, the inner patterns were usually made from fired clay.

These negative core passage patterns were set in the sand mold, carefully aligned and then cemented in place. Often, twenty-odd patterns would be used to form the inside of a cylinder head.

Along with the patterns, venting and pouring passages—called sprues—had to be set into the sand. The pouring cavity was usually sited at the center of the mold so the molten metal would flow easily in both directions to completely fill the casting. Several venting sprues were essential to allow the displaced air from the incoming metal an exit port, and were located at strategic points at corners of the mold. In addition, the wet sand steamed when the hot metal was poured, and the venting sprues provided an escape passage for the moisture.

With the mold and sprues set, the male and female halves of the metal trays were joined and locked in place. The molten metal was poured into the mold and left to cool for about an hour. When the

Ferrari foundry, Maranello, 1979
The work system in the foundry was reorganized in the 1960s or 1970s to match the increase in Ferrari production. Now, the molds traveled along the roller lines—in a sort of assembly line for casting work. The worker at center was heating preformed molds so they would be up to temperature before the alloy was poured. Through the years, Ferrari's foundry also did some commercial casting work for other businesses. *Peter Coltrin, courtesy Road & Track*

Ferrari foundry, Maranello, 1974
It was break time in the foundry. The stacks of freshly cast V-8 engine blocks show off the shine characteristic of sand molds. These castings still bear flashing and the forms of the vents and sprues. Resting atop wooden pallets, the blocks would be transferred to the milling machines in the main factory buildings. *Hilary A. Raab, Jr.*

99

Ferrari foundry, Maranello, 1989
Sand-casting patterns were cleaned for reuse. Most of the foundry's operation was given over to setting up and cleaning molds; the actual pouring and casting of components took up little space.

Ferrari foundry, Maranello, 1989
A worktable with mallets and numbered dies for hammering serial numbers into freshly cast engine blocks was located steps away from the casting machine. Batches of cool blocks were done at a time.

Previous page
Ferrari foundry, Maranello, 1989
The machine for casting V–8 engine blocks. The four walls to the pattern come together in the center. The molten metal was drawn up from furnaces below ground and was poured from the twin-lipped bowl at right rear.

metal had hardened, the trays were unlocked and opened, and the rough casting was extracted. At this point, the casting was an ugly piece of work in comparison with the final machined, faced and polished cylinder head: it was coated in fine sand, metal flashing and the shapes of the sprues.

Colombo engines relied on interference press-fit cylinder sleeves made of cast iron, machined to tolerance; Lampredi engines had screw-in sleeves. These sleeves were used for several reasons. First, the crudity of sand molds made it almost impossible to cast exact tolerances into the engine bores. Second, because of their light weight, aluminum alloy engine blocks were preferred versus cast-iron blocks, but the aluminum was soft in comparison and would not hold up to the pistons' abuse.

The early engines also had freeze plugs cast into the blocks, although Ferrari hardly expected the engines to be subject to freezing. These plug holes were used in the foundry as channels to flush out leftover sand and sludge following the sand casting, a feature typical on sand-cast engine blocks of many marques.

The foundry in the 1990s

In 1989, the work techniques within Ferrari's foundry had changed little since the first foundry opened in 1954. Sand molds were everywhere, laid out for work across the floor, furnaces still glowed with their orange fires. The major advancement in the shop was in terms of organization: for larger-scale production, casting trays for engine and transmission casings were set up on a raised roller line, and a new mechanized casting machine for V–8 engine blocks was at work in another wing of the foundry.

Below the ground floor, the foundry furnaces were stationed. Large melting pots like witches' caldrons sat in the center of the room. Ferrari workers mixed all the alloys in these caldrons, measuring powdered metals with spoons or dropping ingots and bars into the steaming pots. The V–8 and the Testarossa flat-twelve engine casings were made of an aluminum alloy, comprising ninety percent aluminum and 9.4 percent silicon. The remaining 0.6 percent was composed of trace amounts of titanium, magnesium, manganese, copper and iron.

On the ground floor, the centerpiece of the foundry was the mechanized die-casting machine with four-sided tooled molds for the V–8 engine blocks. These molds were made of metal and contained all the core passages preformed into their walls; no subpatterns or sand molds needed to be fussed with. The metal molds were heated up so they would not crack with the sudden addition of molten metal, and then lubricated so the poured aluminum would not bond with the mold. The liquid aluminum alloy was drawn up from the basement furnaces and poured into the molds at approximately 600 degrees Centigrade, or 1,272 degrees Fahrenheit—six times the boiling point of water.

After cooling, the four sides of the mold were pulled back and the glistening engine block was left standing. The block was hoisted by overhead crane to join other newly cast blocks resting on a pallet to the side. A worker armed with mallet and stamps plucked each block from the pallet and punched serial numbers into the fresh metal.

In a corner of the foundry alongside the production car sand-casting works, the race shop had a workbench set up for its foundry

Ferrari foundry, Maranello, 1989
The fresh block was lifted away from the casting machine by a hoist and set in a metal case with other blocks. The box was full here, so blocks rested on the floor.

operation. Workers formed the sand into the metal mold trays, and magnesium alloy was poured from a smelting caldron. Once cooled, the brown Electron castings were cleaned of sand at the worktable. A finished Formula One differential case was loaded into a basket on the rear of a bicycle and the young worker in his blue Ferrari coveralls pedaled away from the foundry, through the factory gates and on over to the race shop for machining.

Chapter 5

Engine Assembly
Breathing Life Into Metal

The spirit and work techniques involved in assembling a Ferrari engine—whether a V–8 or Testarossa Boxer twelve in the 1990s—remained much the same throughout Ferrari's forty years of race car and sports car building. Meanwhile, all other assembly and build procedures at Maranello evolved or advanced. The production of cars grew from one-off fabrication to assembly line construction and on to the verges of mass production with the 308 GTB series in the 1980s. Foundry work became mechanized with automated mold-forming machines to die-cast V–8 engine blocks. Through all the changes at Ferrari, the building of engines changed the least.

On one hand, Ferrari came close to getting the engine right the first time, versus making scores of advances and modifications to chassis, brakes, suspensions, transmissions, engine layout and so on over the years. Enzo Ferrari was the great conservative of racing. For the most part, he stood by the tried and true, developing versus changing, and changing only when he was losing races to novel technology. Brakes were revolutionized in the late 1950s when Jaguar showed the future, being the last to brake into each corner at Le Mans thanks to its revolutionary Girling discs; Ferrari was forced, grudgingly, to soon follow suit. The engine layout needed to win races changed from front-engined cars to mid-engined cars at the dawn of the 1960s; again, Ferrari was bound to keep up with the competition and the times. With his V–12 engine of 1946, Ferrari was the revolutionary, hurling a challenge at the racing establishment. Still, Ferrari chose to develop the engine through the years rather than change it.

On the other hand, assembling an engine is assembling an engine. Ferrari Automobili's stepparent company, Fiat, not only showed the world how machines, computers and robots could build cars, it also built the machines, computers and robots for other mass-production car manufacturers. At Scaglietti and Pininfarina, automated stamping

Ferrari factory, Maranello, 1989
An engine neared completion. Engine assemblers such as Lorenzo Dre stood on their feet all day long building the motors. The job was not hurried, although the engine moved along the line at set intervals and the work was supposed to be completed at the finish of the cycle. Assemblers were taught to gauge their time in constructing the engines, and a supervisor came around to check on progress only rarely.

Ferrari factory, Maranello, 1989
British-made Eaton valves for the Testarossa engine builders were stored loosely in cardboard boxes. When it came time for them to be set into the cylinder heads, the worker simply reached into the box for a handful.

Ferrari factory, Maranello, circa 1960
This publicity photograph showed the engine dynamometer test room with five test beds visible. The engines on the first two dynamometers appeared to be Tipo 156 double overhead cam Formula Ones mounted with three twin downdraft Webers. The engine on the central dynamometer appeared to be a 250 Testa Rossa, and a 250 GT production car engine was on the back dynamometer. *Ferrari S.p.A., courtesy Museo dell'Automobile Carlo Biscaretti di Ruffia*

presses and mechanized spot welders can be used to shape and form body styling with one worker merely guiding the process. And at Ferrari itself, grinding lathes can finish forged crankshafts and camshafts based on preset computer programs; people are needed only to program the computer and load the forgings into the mouth of the machine. Engines, however, require the human touch. Even at Fiat, one of the world's most automatized automobile makers, building engines requires hands-on work.

Building a Ferrari engine is half-magic, breathing life into the cold mass of aluminum and steel. Young Lorenzo Dre built Testarossa flat-twelve engines at Maranello in 1989. Dre was dwarfed by the monstrous bulk of the Redhead perched on its stand, wrapped in ignition wires and topped by glistening cast-aluminum intake manifolds. He spoke as he worked: "In the long run, making the motors is really only an assemblage of components, but there is a part that is artisanship and for that part I do the job happily."

The soul of the Ferrari

Enzo Ferrari was always a practical man, yet when he spoke of his V–12 engines, he became mystical. "Engines have a soul," he eulogized

Ferrari factory, Maranello, 1958
In this view from the other end, the machining shop had been cleaned up for a publicity photograph. Finished V–12 engine blocks sat on the floor at bottom center. *Peter Coltrin Collection, courtesy Hilary A. Raab, Jr.*

in his memoirs. In conversation with Italian journalist Gino Rancati, he could only use metaphor: "Engines are like sons: one settles down and studies, and another signs checks and is dissolute." Even in his remembrance of drivers past, *Piloti, che gente . . . ,* Ferrari couldn't resist mentioning his engines: "the crowning glory of my ambitions."

Ferrari wrote that the inspiration for a twelve-cylinder engine came from his childhood. He recalled the impression an American V–12 Packard had on him—the smooth mechanical operation, muscular horsepower, ample torque and, above all, glorious sound. Up to that point, V–12 engines had been largely used in cars such as the Packard—refined, exclusive and expensive luxury touring cars. A handful of race cars had been powered by V–12 engines before World War II, notably the early Delage and the 1938–39 Mercedes-Benz W163. Still, the suitability and reliability of the V–12 for racing was in its infancy, largely unproven. Emerging from World War II with limited capital to set the foundation for his firm's future, Ferrari had little room for error. To wager all on a V–12 must have required a leap of faith.

The V–12 engines Ferrari was probably the most versed in came from his apprenticeship days racing with Alfa Romeo. The company's engineers created several twelve-cylinder race engines of differing designs in the prewar years—most of them short-lived.

The Portello twelve-cylinder engines came from the drawing board of chief designer Wilfredo Ricart; Ferrari held the Spaniard's

Ferrari factory, Maranello, 1952
Early milling of the Ferrari V–12 engine blocks followed the sand casting. From floor level, the machine tools shop was crowded and certainly loud, with workers wearing no ear or eye protection. An uncleaned block rested at far right, still coated with sand residue from the molds. *Road & Track*

work in such low regard that Ferrari would soon quit Alfa Corse. Along with his later extravagant flat-twelve Tipo 512 and Tipo 162 135 degree V–16 engines, Ricart and fellow designer Bruno Trevisan produced in 1938 the V–12 S10. Ferrari engine designer Gioacchino Colombo had worked alongside Ricart at Alfa Romeo, and the fundamentals of Colombo's Tipo 125 Ferrari V–12 followed those of the S10: twelve cylinders set in a 60–degree V, with a single overhead camshaft for each cylinder bank. From there, the designs diverged.

Ferrari wrote in his memoirs that he conceived of his V–12 engine during the war, before the days of Ferrari Automobili when work was concentrated on machine tools. In a clever bit of detective work, historian Hans Tanner reported on an early factory Tipo 125 blueprint for a Ferrari slipper-type rocker arm: the blueprint was dated October

29, 1946, and the company logo on the page was that of Auto Avio Costruzioni, before Ferrari's founding. Tanner concluded that the general engine layout must have been finished well before that date, as the rocker arm was a small detail in the overall design.

The Colombo V–12 engine established Ferrari. The design had its faults and compromises, yet through constant development and modifications, the engine continued to power Ferraris up through the 365 GTB/4 of 1973. But this engine was suited to sports cars and GT cars; for the given 1.5 liter displacement, it could not match the power of the Tipo 158 Alfetta on the Grand Prix circuits. Thus, in 1949, Colombo's assistant and eventual successor, Aurelio Lampredi, designed a highly modified version of the Colombo V–12. Lampredi's new engine used a big-block casting with screw-in cylinder liners and eliminated the

Ferrari factory, Maranello, 1989
Aptly named Green Giants milling machines and their supporting lines of engine castings to be machined. Ferrari's Flexible Machining System worked 24 hours a day, and each unit produced approximately 24 completed engine blocks in that period—one block per hour.

Ferrari factory, Maranello, 1989
Overhead view of a computerized mill. The casting to be machined was mounted on the turntable plinth at center, and the various machines at each side moved in to do their work. The machine automatically selected bits from the rack at right, based on the preset program for machining castings.

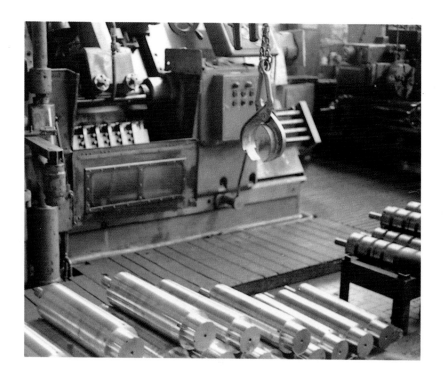

troublesome head gaskets. The cylinder bores were also spaced farther apart, allowing for increased displacement. On July 14, 1951, a Lampredi-engined Ferrari Tipo 375 beat the Alfa Romeos.

The Colombo and Lampredi V-12s powered Ferrari into the 1970s. Nevertheless, the company experimented and won races with numerous other engines that undeservedly remained in the shadows of the V-12 engines' glory as Ferrari in fact has not won a Formula One World Championship with a V-12 car! As early as 1952, an inline four-cylinder double overhead cam engine was used in Ferrari Formula One cars, and Alberto Ascari won the 1952 and 1953 World Championships in a four-cylinder Ferrari. In 1955, inline six-cylinder engines appeared in sports racers, and by 1958, Dino Ferrari's V-6 engines were proving their worth. As of 1990, Ferrari's road and race laurels rested on the strength of the V-8 in the Mondial, 348, F40 and

Ferrari factory, Maranello, 1974

Ferrari was always proud of its crankshafts—even to the point of showing off the whole crankshaft construction process in its 1968–69–70 Annual. Fresh steel billets, left, awaited the hoist to move them onto the lathe. The unworked solid steel billet weighed in at 149 kg, or 328 lb. Following the machining, magnafluxing, heat treating and nitriding, the finished crankshaft weighed 55 lb. *Hilary A. Raab, Jr.*

Valve Springs and Engine Design: Building a Better Mousetrap

When Gioacchino Colombo designed the first Ferrari V-12 engine in 1946, he chose hairpin, or mousetrap, valve springs to close the valves, with two springs per valve. The benefits of the mousetrap springs were shorter valve stems, which slightly reduced the reciprocating valve weight, and a lower-profile cylinder head valve cover, which reduced engine weight, also allowing for a slightly smaller exterior engine dimension. The Aurelio Lampredi designed big-block V-12 continued this feature.

A major drawback to this design was that only three cylinder head studs could be accommodated around each cylinder. When these early V-12s were run hard, they often blew head gaskets, as the three studs weren't able to maintain a tight fit between head, gasket and block.

A secondary drawback to the Colombo cylinder head design, not necessarily related to the valve springs, was the use of siamesed intake ports. This feature was acceptable for the early engines because the sport engines used a single downdraft Weber carburetor and the Grand Prix engines were supercharged; thus, individual intake port tuning wasn't essential.

As Ferrari cars were pushed harder in competition, these problems needed addressing. During production of the Tipo 225 in 1952, beginning around car serial number 0170ET, roller cam followers replaced the finger followers in the Colombo V-12 engine (the Lampredi big-block V-12 had used roller followers from the start). There is no evidence that rollers became the norm at that time, however, as some subsequent engines still had finger followers.

In 1957, some 250 Testa Rossas were seen with the spark plugs moved outside the heads, rather than inside in the V as before. These engines still had the hairpin valve springs, but Ferrari was looking for

something to replace them because they weren't as reliable as the rest of the engine.

When Phil Hill came back to California between the 1957 and 1958 competition seasons, he brought blueprints for a new Ferrari 250 GT V-12 cylinder head design. This new head would feature coil valve springs, individual intake ports, spark plugs located on the outside of the head and four studs around each cylinder.

Hill went straight to Art Sparks, owner of the ForgedTrue Piston Company in Pasadena, California. In his biographical book *Speedway,* Sparks remembered it this way: "Phil brought in a set of blueprints and we got to work on it, although it wasn't easy; I learned a lot from working with Ferrari. Those were lock-out type springs, with no valve cups, just a guide and threaded cam follower on the end of the valve for clearance adjustment and to take the thrust of the valve. We made them a sealed spring with a titanium seat dampener, for that beautiful twelve cylinder engine."

Sparks found that the best spring wire was made in Sweden, so he bought a large supply of wire, which he took to a spring-winding specialist in Detroit, Michigan. The first Ferrari to benefit from these new coil valve springs was the 1958 Testa Rossa, and the shop made the coil valve springs for all Ferrari V-12 engines for the next five years.

The new cylinder head design was gradually phased into production road cars as well as competition cars in the ensuing few years. This made the engine not only more powerful and reliable, but easier to work on. Dean Batchelor remembered that when he changed the spark plugs on his 1958 Boano-Ellena 250 GT coupe the first time, it took an hour and a half. By the time he'd owned the car three years, he had halved the time to forty-five minutes. The twelve plugs on the newer engine could be changed in fifteen minutes or less—with far less chance of cross-threading the plugs, which was a constant worry on the inside-plug engines.

Formula One cars, and on the flat-twelve in the Testarossa. In the interim, Ferrari experimented with designs as different as Lampredi's 1953 Tipo 116 inline 2493 cc two-cylinder Grand Prix engine and the Tipo 318W 2986 cc engine, with its eighteen cylinders arranged in three banks forming a W.

The first engines

In constructing sports and race cars, Ferrari was always an assembler despite his goal of building as many components as feasible in-house. The chassis, suspension and bodywork for most early cars were almost entirely built by subcontractors, but with his engines Ferrari came the closest to meeting his aim.

On speculation, there are several reasons Ferrari would have had such a goal. First, he was going racing, and he would have preferred to protect his engineering secrets from others—whether they be in engine casting design or in the way a double-shear suspension joint was constructed. These secrets won races and provided Ferrari Automobili its livelihood.

Ferrari factory, Maranello, 1989
Rows of lathes for fabricating Ferrari crankshafts. In the large pale green machines at bottom, the bulk of the work was done by automation.

Ferrari factory, Maranello, 1989
Fine polishing of the crankshafts was done on a polisher, requiring the human touch to work up the mirror finish on journals.

Ferrari factory, Maranello, 1989
Finished V–8 engine crankshafts ready for delivery to the engine builders were stored on wheeled carts. Similar carts were used to store and transfer camshafts.

Second, by fabricating components in-house, Ferrari could control his sought-after quality and reliability. In the years following World War II, quality subcontractors for building race cars must have been difficult to come by, as the economy was concerned primarily with resurrecting the country, not racing cars and motorcycles. Thus, Ferrari may have been forced to construct some components that he would have preferred to purchase.

Finally, there was Enzo Ferrari's pride. Building his own race car with his own components was better than sharing the glory.

For the first Colombo Tipi 125, 159 and 166 engines constructed by Ferrari Automobili in 1946–49, it was difficult to ascertain which parts were fabricated by Ferrari and which were subcontracted. The early engines used blocks, cylinder heads, timing cases and oil sumps cast by Calzoni from an aluminum-copper alloy that was easy to work, light in weight and resilient. Cylinder liners were of a hard iron, probably cast by Calzoni as well.

For the crankshaft, a solid steel billet was machined on grinders and lathes, probably within the factory. Although machined crankshafts may not be as strong as forged units, the economy of scale for

Ferrari factory, Maranello, circa 1975
Ferrari camshafts emerged from the heat-treating furnace red-hot. *Hilary A. Raab, Jr.*

Ferrari factory, Maranello, 1989
Camshaft machinist Marcello Besagna operated the automated milling machines, run on computer-programmed cycles. Like the crankshafts, the camshafts were milled from forged steel. After the basic milling on the machine, the finer finishing work was performed by hand. Coming out of the machine, one of every few camshafts was miked to ensure quality control. Besagna, 25 years old, had worked in the factory since he was 16. Like most employees, he was *"apassionato della Ferrari."*

112

Ferrari factory, Maranello, 1989
The cam lobe lifts for V–8 engine camshafts were tested in a handmade box. The dial indicators read the measurements as a camshaft was rotated.

Ferrari factory, Maranello, 1989
Fine polishing of camshaft lobes required a deft touch with a hand-held electric grinder. Vacuum pipes were to suck away metal dust. Yellow racks of camshafts waited at right corner.

limited production forced Ferrari to use machining. Ferrari's pride in its machined crankshafts had remained strong throughout the years; in the 1968-69-70 Annual, eleven pages were diverted from the racing review to showcase how the crankshafts were made at Maranello. Each V-12 crankshaft required seventeen hours of machining over sixty-five working days. The unworked solid steel billet weighed in at 149 kg, or 328 lb. Following the machining, magnafluxing, heat treating and nitriding, the finished crankshaft weighed 25 kg, or 55 lb. Historian Hans Tanner stated that the crankshafts in the first Colombo engines went through a similar weight reduction: from 225 kg, or 500 lb, to 22.5 kg, or 50 lb, ten percent of the original.

Colombo ran up against a major engineering hurdle in terms of bearings to support the crankshaft mains and the connecting rods. Finding quality bearings for racing in the late 1940s and early 1950s was difficult at best based on the era's metallurgy and the alloys

Ferrari factory, Maranello, 1989
Final preparation of V-8 cylinder heads before polishing. Prepared heads rested everywhere: on workbenches, on wooden pallets and directly on the floor.

Ferrari factory, Maranello, 1989
A row of the green booths lined a far wall in the factory, provided with ample natural light and fluorescent lamps for the polishing job. Armed with electric grinders, workers polished V-8 cylinder heads to a mirror finish while the heads were held in a specially built vise. Eye and ear protection were mandatory.

Ferrari factory, Maranello, 1989
Fresh from the Green Giants milling machines were V-8 cylinder heads, foreground, and Testarossa engine crankcase halves, background. The heads waited to be hauled to the other end of the factory for fine machining and polishing.

114

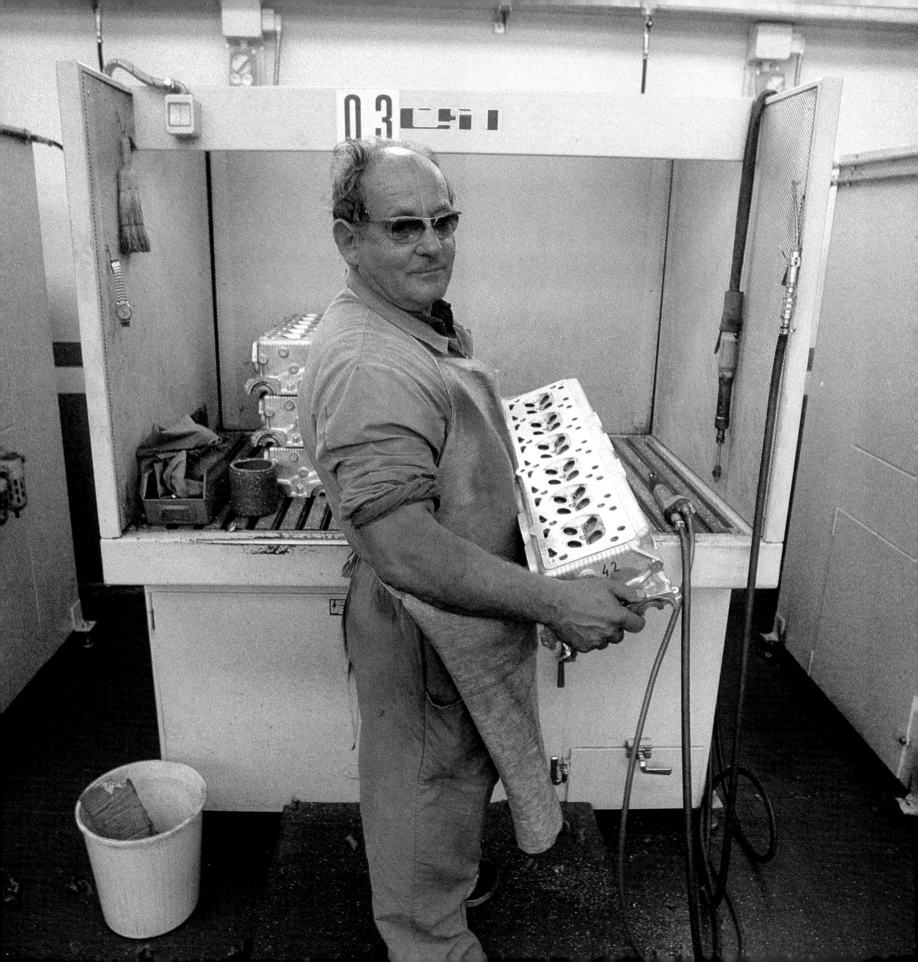

Ferrari factory, Maranello, 1989
Veteran engine polisher Remo Albergucci showed off the finished job; a gleaming Testarossa head with six cylinders on the bank, each with four valves.

available. Ferrari finally came upon the English Vandervell-built American-designed Clevite thin-wall bearings made of lead-indium backed with an aluminum alloy. The Vandervell bearings were expensive but essential components and played an important role in Ferrari's future successes.

Pistons, connecting rods and valves were almost certainly bought in parts. Ignition was supplied by dual Marelli magnetos, at first mounted horizontally at each end of the block. Weber carburetors in several setups provided fuel intake.

Perhaps the most fascinating aspect of the early engines—and the cars as a whole—was in a small yet important component. The heads of bolts used throughout the engines and chassis of Ferrari's even-numbered race cars and odd-numbered road cars built from 1947 through 1949 bore a prancing horse image in relief. The Prancing Horse bolts were either made for Ferrari by a fastener supplier or die-cut within the factory itself. If made at Maranello, as appears to be the case, the bolts were evidence of Enzo Ferrari's fastidious commit-

Ferrari factory, Maranello, 1989
A group of V–8 cylinder heads were readied for the addition of the twin overhead camshafts. Camshaft caps and bearings were first assembled for fit and then reassembled and torqued for final assembly.

Ferrari factory, Maranello, 1989
With the camshaft in place on a V–8 engine cylinder head, the nuts were hand tightened into place before final assembly. Standard procedure for engine building included preassembly of many components to test fit. The components were then often moved on to another work station where final assembly was done.

Ferrari factory, Maranello, 1989
Cylinder heads were inspected before engine assembly. Factory workers wore blue *tuta* overalls with the Ferrari emblem above the heart; technical inspectors wore brown coats, again with the Ferrari emblem.

Ferrari factory, Maranello, 1989
Valve seats were inserted in a V–8 cylinder head by hand with the help of a press. This job required a fine touch to know when seats were properly set.

117

ment to controlling the quality of his cars' components; fabricating the bolts would have required an immense amount of labor-intensive, time-consuming work. Either way, by 1949, Ferrari was purchasing bolts as well as other fasteners from OEB, or Officine Egidio Brugola, based in Lissone, outside Milan; Enzo Ferrari gave thanks to OEB in

his 1949 Annual. Nevertheless, throughout its history, Ferrari continued to fabricate a small number of its own specialty fasteners for race cars.

Machining engine components in the 1990s

A huge portion of the Maranello works in the 1990s was devoted to casting, machining, polishing, finishing and, finally, assembling Ferrari engines.

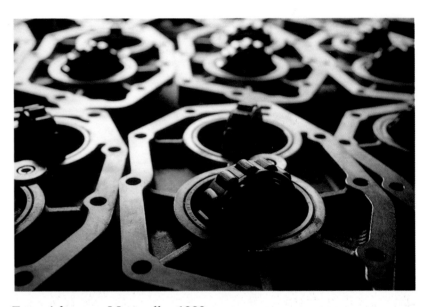

Ferrari factory, Maranello, 1989
Caged cylindrical bearings for the transmissions rested on a shelf ready for assembly.

Ferrari factory, Maranello, 1989
Alongside the Testarossa engine assembly area, V–8 production car gearboxes were built. The process was almost as time-consuming and intricate as that of constructing the engines. Casings were set on a worktable and assembled by hand with parts from the stock shelves in the background.

Ferrari factory, Maranello, 1989
The first stage in preparing gear case covers for assembly was to add locating studs for final construction. Special clamps held the cases in place on the workbench.

Coming from the foundry, cast pieces such as the engine block, cylinder heads, sump and so on were carted on old wooden pallets by forklift to a newer wing built off the old triangular factory. Here, Fiat's influence on Ferrari was most evident: Ferrari's Flexible Machining System, a long line of Green Giants, the automated, computer-controlled engine-block machining mills. The machines were primarily by Mandelli, built in Piacenza; the bank of operating computers rested overhead on a balcony.

Ferrari claimed this to be the most modern machining system of its kind when construction began in 1983. The mills ran twenty-four hours a day and could be operated by one worker.

A preprogrammed drill was at the center of each mill, set within one of the green-painted work booths that gave the machines their name. The drill selected its bits automatically from an overhead chain-driven rack, alternating tools as the machining process continued. The block or other casting to be machined rested on a turntable plinth that revolved as the computer dictated. Approximately one hour— more or less depending on the casting—was needed on the mill to produce the finished piece.

During the day, samples of the castings were constantly taken from the mills to worktables, where their tolerances were checked by hand with the aid of a dial micrometer. If one tolerance was off, the

Ferrari factory, Maranello, 1989
Transaxle rear differential gears awaited assembly. With the stress on assembly-line-style production, such organization as keeping parts shelves well stocked was an essential lesson for Ferrari to learn under Fiat's guidance.

Ferrari factory, Maranello, 1989
The assembly area for the Testarossa engines was quiet, but the building of the transmissions was even more silent. Most of the gearbox was handbuilt piece by piece without preassembled subcomponents arriving from other parts of the factory. Assemblers worked largely by themselves in building the units.

Ferrari factory, Maranello, 1989
A set of eight V–8 connecting rods and pistons was laid out on the worktable and the wrist pins were fitted with light taps from the mallet. Here, circlips were added to retain the pins. The tool? A Phillips screwdriver. Few women were employed on the assembly lines themselves; most worked in the foundry or the finishing shop. The first women employees were hired at Ferrari in 1967; as of 1989, some 150 women worked within the factory.

mill's work was suspect and the machine was shut down pending reprogramming.

Finished cylinder heads were carried by forklift to a series of booths set against a back wall where polishing and porting work was performed. A line of aproned men armed with fine-stone machine polishers worked over the heads with quick and practiced motions. Vacuums in the booths sucked away debris.

Although almost all the castings were poured and finished in the factory, the crankshafts and camshafts were an exception. Forged by a specialized subcontractor in KNV steel, the crankshafts and camshafts for the V–8 and Boxer twelve engines were then trucked to the factory and machined on miniature versions of the Green Giants. Even though castings were checked at regular intervals within the production, every crankshaft and camshaft was tolerance-tested with micrometers throughout the process.

Building the Testarossa flat-twelve Tipo F113A

From the mechanized roar and rush of workers on the two main assembly lines for the V–8 engined 308 GTB series, Mondial t and first of the 348 series, the tiny engine assembly sector where the Tipo F113A Testarossa flat-twelve engines were constructed was a step into another world. The engine assembly area was silent. Here people worked at a craft. They took joy in the job; their silence was due to their concentration.

The Testarossa engine assembly area bordered the two main assembly lines and was across the isle from a large sector marked off for building the numerous V–8 road car engines. The V–8 engine area showed the same signs of absorption in the work, but owing to the sheer volume of production it was noisy and busy. The limited run of F40 twin turbocharged V–8 engines was built in a sectioned-off part of the general V–8 assembly area.

Testarossa engines were built in a small U-shaped area defined by shelving laden with components—from nuts and bolts to stacks of the red crinkle-finish cam covers that gave the Testarossa and its elder sibling, the 1957 model 250 Testa Rossa, their names. No more than twenty people worked in the sector, constructing the mammoth engines.

Set back from the actual engine assembly was a series of worktables where subcomponents of the engine were put together. At one table, the cylinder heads were built up. A man collected together twenty-four of the cast-iron valve seats for the six cylinders in each head. He located seats with the gentle tap of a wooden mallet, checking the fit of each seat with his fingers; only by touch and sound could the work be done correctly.

Valves were assembled in place, the man gathering loose ones from a cardboard box set under the workbench. The valves for the

Ferrari factory, Maranello, 1989
In the first stage of assembling a Testarossa flat-twelve engine, an engine builder trainee moved half a crankcase into place with help from an electric overhead hoist. The crankcase was then bolted to the engine stand for assembly. This apprentice was in his early 20s and had spent time constructing V–8 engines before moving up to the Boxer line. An experienced Testarossa engine builder divided his time between assembling an engine and teaching this newcomer.

Ferrari factory, Maranello, 1989
The finished piston-and-connecting-rod assemblies were stored in batches with their base caps in wooden crates awaiting the engine builder.

Ferrari factory, Maranello, 1989
With the piston well coated in oil, a sleeve was slid around it, holding the compression and oil rings. The connecting rod was then backed into the engine block and the piston pushed through the sleeve and into the cylinder. A couple gentle taps with a mallet handle finished the job. Next, the connecting rod caps were fitted, nuts hand tightened onto the connecting rod bolts and torqued in place. With all 12 pistons inserted, the crankshaft was rotated several times to check its throw and the smooth operation of the pistons in the cylinders.

Ferrari factory, Maranello, 1989
Working between a cart bearing the wooden crate of piston-and-connecting-rod assemblies and an engine block on a stand, a Testarossa engine builder liberally soaked a piston in assembly oil with the help of a paintbrush. The battered paint can held the assembly oil. Connecting rod nuts waited next to the can on the cart top. This worker was not wearing his blue Ferrari *tuta* overalls; as one worker stated, "You can wear what you want but you must have a Ferrari insignia above your chest for identification." Most workers did wear the overalls, however, and on rare occasions when photographs were taken within the factory, workers were normally required to wear them.

Ferrari factory, Maranello, 1989
A young engine builder laced the wiring for a Testarossa. Typically, engine builders and many other skilled workers within the factory went to a mechanic school such as the Dino Ferrari school in Maranello. The Ferrari school trained workers particularly on the basics of Ferrari engines, although many graduates found work at other auto makers such as Lamborghini and Maserati along with Ferrari. Courses lasted five years: two years were in basic mechanical skill; the final three years were elective, concentrating on specialization. Most assembly line workers came to the factory from the Maranello-Modena region; engineers and skilled mechanics often came from the breadth of Italy. Other mechanics came to the Ferrari school from around the world to brush up on Ferrari skills or in hopes of earning a berth on the Formula One mechanic team.

Ferrari factory, Maranello, 1989
Ferrari factory engine builder Lorenzo Dre's tools included power socket drives, assorted open-end wrenches, T-neck sockets, regular and needle-nose pliers, and the ubiquitous hammer. Masking tape was for covering open engine passages to protect them from outside elements during construction. The pot at left with the brush was filled with silicone paste for lubricating rubber hoses before working them into place. The boxes held selections of nuts, bolts and washers. Dre was obviously a Juventus football team fan.

Ferrari factory, Maranello, 1989

In the U-shaped Testarossa engine assembly area, engines were mounted on the rolling stands, complete with drip tray set below. The stands were moved forward at seven intervals of 84 minutes each whether the assembly task had been completed or not. If it had not been, it was simply done at the next stage. The shape of the area was designated by the shelves and drawers full of engine components from wiring to nuts and bolts. In the background, the twin V–8 production car lines were visible.

Testarossa came from the English Eaton firm, one of the few non-Italian Ferrari parts suppliers. Springs and seals were then added.

The worker selected a pair of the camshafts for each head, laying them in place and bolting down the caps. Finished as a subcomponent, the cylinder head was sent over to the engine assemblers.

Nearby at another worktable, a woman fitted pistons to connecting rods, inserting wrist pins through the piston into the rod's little end and pushing circlips in place with the aid of a Phillips screwdriver. Pistons and connecting rods were assembled in groups of twelve, then set into wooden boxes to be safely stacked up and moved to the builders.

Typically, a Testarossa engine was assembled by one worker, unless a more skilled assembler was teaching an apprentice. On the V–8 engine assembly line, builders worked in pairs at some of the stations.

To begin, the two halves of the bare flat-twelve crankcase were moved into place on a wheeled engine assembly stand. Although the aluminum crankcase halves were not inordinately heavy, workers used overhead machine hoists to lift them. The cases were bolted to the stand, which could be rotated 360 degrees on the horizontal axis for

Ferrari factory, Maranello, 1989
A shelf was full of aluminum alloy valve cover oil breather tubes, piled together like snakes.

reaching any part of the engine. The bearings were set in place and the heavy steel crankshaft was then slid into the crankcase. Aligned, the case was bolted together down its centerline.

The pistons and connecting rods were taken from their wooden storage box one by one, dabbed with a paintbrush of assembly oil and guided into place backward down the cylinder bore, the worker reaching through from the other side of the crankcase to feel the connecting rod into place against the crankshaft. The bolts from the bottom half of the connecting rod were then torqued, and the next piston was inserted. With all the pistons in place, the assembler gave several joyous twists to the crankshaft to check that the crankshaft and pistons moved freely without binding or drag.

The cylinder head was hoisted in place on top of the head gasket, red cam covers were bolted down, manifolds and fuel injectors were

Ferrari factory, Maranello, 1989
Fluids were circulated through a finished Testarossa before sending the engine onto the dynamometers in the test rooms. Fluid pressure was checked and any leaks spotted. Here, 12 year veteran Ferrari engine builder Modesto Pinotti checked the location of the alternator and the stretch of the alternator belt. All such tolerances were adjusted on the assembly line, and the engine was delivered to the test bed ready to run, with only the addition of fuel and test fluids still required. Pinotti was fond of his position at Ferrari and proud of the product: "I say that it is one of the best factories that you could work for. The administration, the department foremen, the atmosphere—everybody gets along. You work hard but it is enjoyable and fulfilling."

Ferrari factory, Maranello, 1989
Lorenzo Dre routed the plumbing atop a Testarossa engine. All hardware for constructing the engine was close at hand in the walls of trays surrounding the work area. Assemblers merely collected the parts they needed as they went along with the job.

Ferrari factory, Maranello, 1989
Building the Redhead, the Testarossa flat-twelve engine. Engine builder Lorenzo Dre was framed by stacks of crinkle-finish Testarossa valve covers.

added, the electrics and ancillaries were attached. The transmission and differential units were assembled on another line and were mated to the bottom of the engine at the end of the line.

The engines were moved along the U-shaped assembly line in seven stages at intervals of eighty-four minutes. Workers appeared to follow the time schedule nonchalantly. If the job was not finished at one stage, the engine was still moved along and the job was finished as it went. If the engine was not finished by the end of the line, the line was held up until the job was done. One to two Testarossa engines were assembled each day.

By the finish, the engine mounted atop the stand had grown from a shiny bare crankcase casting into a sculpture of metal. The bulk of the engine and the dull glow of the curved aluminum intake manifolds spoke of horsepower even before the engine had been sparked to life. In the drip pan carried below the engine on the stand were odd bits of wire ends, dropped washers and cigarette butts floating in a pool of oil.

The tools for the job were few. On a bench along the line, one worker's tools were laid out: several open-end and closed-end hand wrenches, an odd handful of needle-nose pliers, an electric power wrench and a sole wooden mallet, used sparingly.

Ferrari factory, Maranello, 1989
Lorenzo Dre was on break. Within the shop rested bare V–8 engine blocks ready for assembly; outside in the alleyways between the factory buildings were parked the finished cars and the F40s awaiting final work. Dre was passionate about building Testarossa engines: "In the long run, making the motors is really only an assemblage of components, but there is a part that is artisanship and for that I do it happily. There are certain stimuli when doing the job and I have to say that I really enjoy it." On average, one Testarossa engine was constructed each day in the assembly area.

Ferrari factory, Maranello, 1989
A wall of component boxes ran along the Testarossa engine assembly line. All parts were clearly marked, well stocked and easily accessible.

Each completed Testarossa and V–8 engine was broken in with an electric motor powering it before being started on its own. The engine was then run in one of the factory's five test dynamometers for four hours. To loosen up the tight new flat-twelve engine, it was run at 1500 rpm for a time, and gradually warmed up to five-minute bursts at 6000 to 6500 rpm. Maximum horsepower of 390 was reached at 6300 rpm; maximum torque of 361 lb-ft came on at 4500 rpm. The engine was also checked for appropriate fuel consumption, correct oil pressure and consistent temperature readings before being approved for installation.

A thorough twelve-hour endurance test on the dynamometer was given to one engine in a dozen to double-check quality control. Problems were rare.

Ferrari factory, Maranello, 1979
A Boxer twelve on the test bed nearby the engine assembly areas. Destined for a 512 BB, the engine would be run on one of the factory's five dynamometers for four hours at 1500 rpm, warming up to five-minute bursts at 6000 rpm with checks for fuel consumption, oil pressure and consistent temperature readings before being approved for installation. Note the welded-up exhaust manifold and the stainless steel braided fluid lines. *Peter Coltrin, courtesy Road & Track*

Ferrari factory, Maranello, 1989
Finished and tested F40 V–8 engines waited to be mated with car bodies. The engines sat atop their wheeled stands in a far corner of the building where there was extra room, sharing storage space with a janitor's mop bucket.

Chapter 6

F40 Construction
A Step Back to Tradition

The F40 was designed in 1986 to mark the fortieth anniversary of Enzo Ferrari's automobiles. Factory coded as the F120, it celebrated Ferrari's history and at the same time revived much of that history in terms of its own production techniques.

When Enzo Ferrari proposed the concept of the F40 to the Ferrari executive committee on June 6, 1986, he suggested a car that carried on the tradition of the sports racer 250 LM, last built in 1965. In 1964,

Ferrari made an official exit from factory-sponsored and -entered GT racing, and in 1973, Ferrari exited from prototype racing to concentrate solely on Formula One. The new car would return Ferrari to its sports racing roots and celebrate its nine Le Mans victories. More important, the F40 would incorporate much of the new technology used by the factory's Formula One team, technology that had gone largely unused by its current V–8 road cars.

At no other time in Ferrari's history had the Gestione Sportiva and the factory been further separated by technology than in the 1980s. Developments in Ferrari Formula One cars in terms of turbocharging and the use of composite construction had left the road cars in the dust. Indeed, much of that technology was not easily translated to the road cars, beyond the special series 288 GTO of 1984–86. Meanwhile, the factory was looking in the other direction. The assembly lines were hustling to produce all the road cars they could to keep up with

Ferrari factory, Maranello, 1989
The beginning of the assembly process for the limited-run F40s. The chassis-body package was trucked in from Scaglietti in Modena and painted at the Ferrari paint shop. The body was then set on a rolling trolley and wheeled to the start of the production line. It had been carefully fitted and assembled at Modena and then taken apart again for the paint booths, although the painters were careful to keep the original panels together to ensure a consistent paint job. After painting, the body was reassembled for the journey across the alley to the assembly area. It was taken apart again at the start of the assembly process, with patches of masking tape noting the car's serial number so the correct doors and lids would be reattached. The separate panels were carried to the end of the assembly line, bypassing the construction process, stacked up until the car was assembled and then reunited with the original body.

Carrozzeria Scaglietti, Modena, 1989
Wheels for the F40 waited in a storage area along the alleyway between the two wings of the Scaglietti works. The tires were mounted on the wheels at Scaglietti but trucked to Maranello to be put on the cars near the middle of the assembly line.

Ferrari factory, Maranello, 1989
The first stage in F40 construction on the Maranello line was affixing the rear Plexiglas windows to the bodywork. The windows were a tight fit—perhaps from design, perhaps owing to dimensions that were slightly off. In either case, the worker spent some 20 minutes mounting the window, tapping it into its final position with the butt end of a mallet. Weather stripping was then added and glued in place.

customer demand for Ferrari's best-selling car ever, the 308 GTB series in all its forms, with more than 12,000 units rolling off the production lines as of 1989.

With the F40, Ferrari renewed the direct relationship between the race shop and the production lines, a relationship that made Ferrari automobiles what they were, beginning with the Tipo 166 and blossoming with the 250 GT series. The F40 boasted no pretensions; it was a sports racing car with few driver amenities, a marriage of racing car and road car in the Ferrari tradition. From the Formula One cars, the F40 took its turbocharging technology, advances in suspension design and, above all, the composite chassis and body construction techniques.

Composite construction

In build techniques, the wing of the Scaglietti workshops devoted to construction of the F40 chassis, bodywork and many components was a world away from the larger wing where the bodywork for the V–8 road cars was produced. In physical distance, the two workshops were separated merely by a narrow alleyway where spare parts for both car series were stored.

The V–8 car wing was all noise, the sound not of the old panel-beaters' hammers but of robotic welders and machine body presses. There were far more industrial machines in the shop than there were workers, and many of the workers' jobs were relegated to pushing

Ferrari factory, Maranello, 1989
The bodywork for the F40 was designed by Pininfarina in Grugliasco, formed and assembled by Scaglietti in Modena, and painted and finished at Ferrari in Maranello. The Disegno di Pininfarina plaque was added onto the car halfway along the Maranello line.

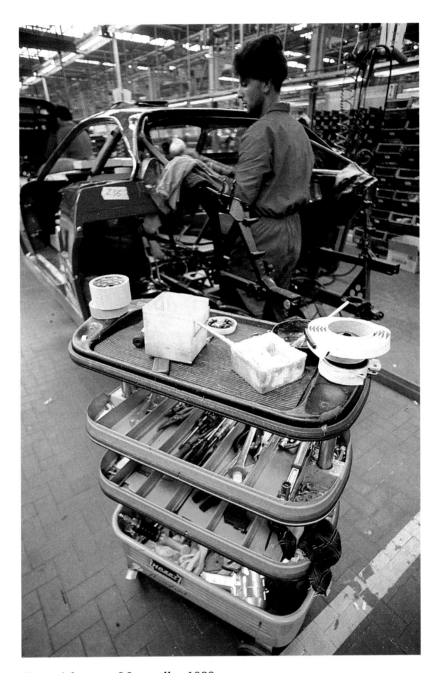

Ferrari factory, Maranello, 1989
Each F40 assembler moved a small cart along with him, or her, carrying tools, adhesive, fasteners and some components. The masking tape affixed to the car's bodywork noted it as car number 236.

buttons. Still, many detail jobs were finished by hand with the use of both electric and hand tools.

In contrast, the F40 shop at Scaglietti was a return to the labor-intensive techniques of chassis and bodywork building that marked all Ferraris until the 1970s. The work required hand-welding of chassis frames, running of glue guns to apply adhesives that held floor pans and the like to the chassis, hand-fitting of body panels to the chassis and final smoothing of the panels with hand files. In terms of work technique, the shop could have been building a 1963 model 250 GTO.

The dividing line lay in the materials. The 250 GTO used an old-fashioned 1960s aluminum body, a chassis made of a steel oval-

section ladder frame and steel space frame, and Plexiglas rear and side windows. The F40 was based on the composite materials that were state of the art in 1980s Formula One racers: an OP 10 steel tube and formed sheet metal chassis, lateral braces of honeycomb aluminum, further braces of Nomex and Kevlar-carbon-fiber weave. Welding techniques for the 250 GTO and F40 chassis were similar, using basic gas welding torches, and were done by hand in both cases. The GTO's aluminum body was worked with hammers and tree stumps to form its

135

Ferrari factory, Maranello, 1989
Front suspension and brake assemblies waited to be added to the F40s on the production line.

Ferrari factory, Maranello, 1989
Following the initial assembly of windows, radiator, shrouds and so on, the F40 body was hoisted to about waist height and driveline components were moved into place. Here, worker Rossano Gibellini bolted the front right suspension-steering unit into place. The unit had arrived at the line pre-assembled from another part of the factory.

Ferrari factory, Maranello, 1989
The car was lowered back onto its wheeled trolley to move on to the next stage of assembly. Riding in the car was Rossano Gibellini, 17 years old, who had worked at Ferrari for approximately six months. Like many Ferrari workers, he was a second-generation employee, as older relatives had started at Maranello in their youth and now had aided him in getting his job. Workers went through a five-year grace period before being granted a permanent position within the works; many had been employed for at least 25 years. In the background, operating the hoist, was Arnaldo Tagliazocchi, a 28 year Ferrari veteran, nicknamed Il nonno—The Grandfather. Paired with the younger worker, it was his job to teach the routine. Asked which cars he had helped construct over the years, Tagliazocchi began counting down from the Testarossa to the different Berlinetta Boxers, the 365 GTB/4—before losing track: "So many that I cannot remember them all," was the final tally.

Ferrari factory, Maranello, 1989
F40 bodies were set on a second platform hoist for the mating of the engine. Here, the engine was lowered into the car's midship bay. The walls of trays were filled with fasteners for use during the assembly process and ample working light came from the overhead skylights that roofed the factory.

Ferrari factory, Maranello, 1989
The empty engine bay of F40 number 234 with rear-wheel-drive axles awaited the gearbox.

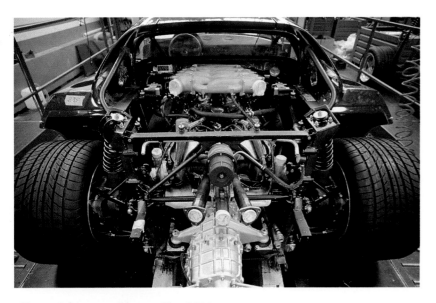

Ferrari factory, Maranello, 1989
Following the addition of the V–8 motor and wheels and tires, the engine bay was filled with hardware. This car, number 235, traveled down the assembly line ahead of its sibling, number 234.

curves; the composite fiber and resin body panels on the F40 were molded in an autoclave. The tooling for the composite molds was much less expensive than similar tooling for pressing the steel bodies of the 308 GTB series. Composite molds were easily altered, allowing flexibility in modifying designs during production, much like the handwork on the 250 GTO. Finishing of the aluminum body and the composite body relied on the same tool: a hand-held file.

Constructing the F40

The assembly line of the F40 at Maranello was an honest attempt at modern production techniques. Cars were in a line and workers had predetermined jobs to be done in a specified order. Cars on the line even moved forward to their next stations at a set interval of forty minutes. Still, as one Ferrari spokesman stated, "We are having many problems with this car."

Some of those problems stemmed simply from the building of the F40. The car was an enigma within the modern Maranello of 1989. It did not fit into the assembly line mode, standing out from the 348 road car lines in both productivity and mindset.

The two side-by-side 348 lines were ablaze in bright white fluorescent lights with a blurr of workers in blue overalls moving around them. The cars ran on a moving line with hoists mechanically lifting them overhead for certain work. These lines were Italian high-tech industrial efficiency incarnate.

Ferrari factory, Maranello, 1989
In this overhead view of the F40 body with the engine in place, worker Claudio Miglioli bolted the rear frame bar into position, supporting the upper shock absorber mounts.

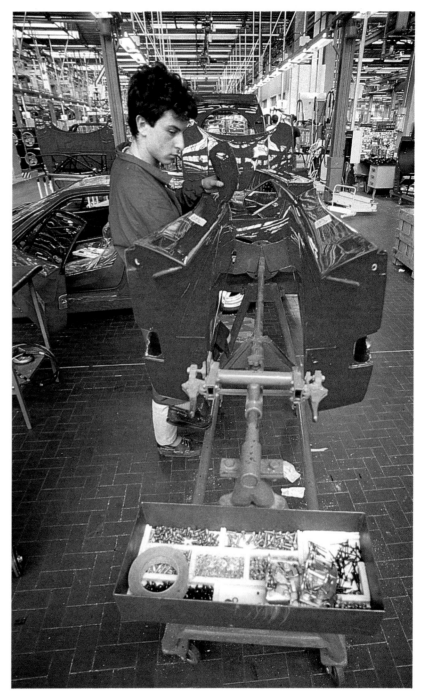

Ferrari factory, Maranello, 1989
Hardware was mounted on a pair of F40 doors, set on a special jig. When the mirrors failed to line up straight, a muscular twist refigured their bodies. The patches of masking tape tell which car body these doors belong to.

Ferrari factory, Maranello, 1989
Connecting wiring and hoses ran from the installed engine to the chassis components. The exhaust system had also been mounted in place, as had the composite rear underbody section. The worker was using an electric drill to put new holes in the chassis framework for the assembly; such modifications on the production line were commonplace with the F40.

141

The F40 line was casual, quiet and slow. No streams of fluorescent track lighting blazed down on the workers and the noise of the mechanized hoists was all in the background. Walking into the assembly area of the F40 was like taking a step back in time.

The F40 assembly area sat off to one side of the dual V–8 road car lines like a waif. The line was slotted in between the true production lines and the Green Giants machines for the engine components. Even the Ferrari spokesman apologized that the line was makeshift, set up only for the limited run of 800 to 900 cars. Nevertheless, spirits on the F40 line were high. The twelve assemblers were building the ultimate Ferrari road car—and they knew it.

The chassis-bodywork package arrived from Modena to be painted at Maranello. It was rolled to the beginning of the line atop wheeled dollies. A total of ten cars moved down the line at one time, with the rate of completion running at 0.8 to 2 cars per day, as the factory reported. From beginning to end—from casting of the engine block and welding up of the chassis through to assembly, road test and final inspection approval for delivery—twenty-five working days went into the fabrication of each F40. At least one full day was needed just to assemble the twin turbocharged V–8 engine.

The first step on the line was the addition of the rear Plexiglas windows to the cockpit, the divider between engine and driver. A worker applied a thin line of adhesive to the composite body and mounted the window in position. The fit was too tight, so he used the butt end of a wooden mallet to force it into place. When he was satisfied, rubber weather stripping was added and glued down with a gun. Total time for the operation: twenty minutes.

Meanwhile, a second worker attached a composite shroud to the dual front radiator fans. The composite piece had been preformed, but as with the rear window, the fit was far from perfect. The worker set the shroud in place and eyeballed the clearances. He then took the shroud to a nearby workbench and used a hand file to enlarge holes. The shroud was set back in place, measured and then returned to the bench for further filing. After four trips back and forth, the fit was correct and the piece was secured in place. Time elapsed: twenty-five minutes.

The detail work continued, and the car moved forward at set forty-minute intervals. Workers followed along, starting or finishing their jobs wherever the car was on the line. The assembly did not follow Henry Ford's classic organization of one man, one bolt.

At stage two, the chassis was lifted off the wheeled dolly by a hoist and elevated so that two workers could get underneath to assemble the suspension and brake units. From there, the chassis was lowered onto a platform lift and an engine was called for. A worker arrived with a V–8 engine on rollers, wheeled forth from a distant corner of the shop

Ferrari factory, Maranello, 1989

This overhead view showed the final stages of the F40 line. The worker at bottom was mounting the turbocharger intercooler in place with the help of an electric socket drive. Further on, the cars were hoisted in the air again for finishing work to the undercarriage and driveline. The production lines for twin V–8 cars were situated at right, running parallel to the F40 line. Behind the wall at left, the Green Giants computerized milling machines were at work.

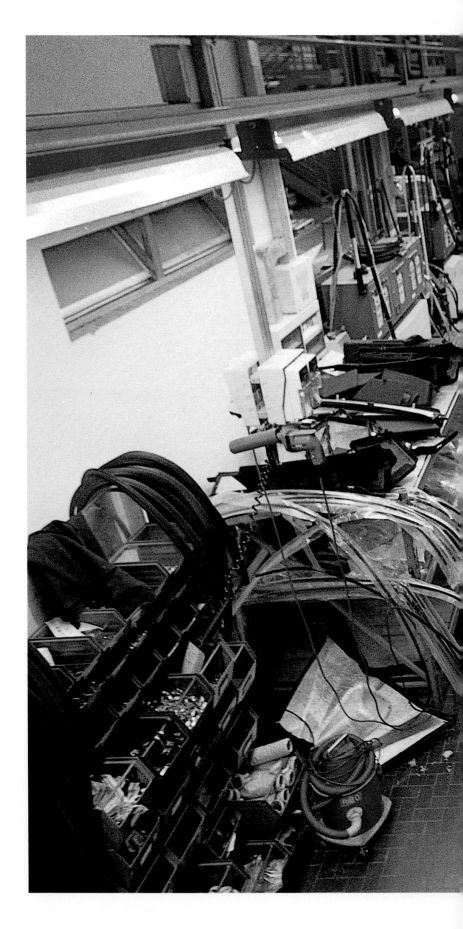

Carrozzeria Scaglietti, Modena, 1989
Bridgestone tires for the F40s waited for mounting at Scaglietti. The finished cars would ride atop Pirellis, but with the Pirelli shipment late, Bridgestones were used in the meantime.

where finished engines were stored. The engine was lifted by hoist and lowered in place, with two workers attaching the mounts from above and below. At the same time, wheels and tires were fitted; with the standard Pirelli P-Zero shipment late, Bridgestone rubber was used.

With the engine in place, the car was lowered onto its own wheels, and from this point to the end of the line it was rolled forward by the strength of a worker or two. The twin turbochargers were bolted in place, with a worker laying across the engine to reach the mounts. Further on, the seats, bare-bones interior, Momo steering wheel and gauges were added by a worker contorted inside the cockpit like Houdini to reach mounting bolts.

The assembly line lost its stages at this point. In some open work space at the end of the line, one of the workers who mounted the engine was at work on the rear hood. The hood was set upside-down on a metal table and the louvered Plexiglas was glued in place. At the first worker's side, another worker had two doors on a jig, adding on mirrors and hardware. When one mirror refused to line up straight, a simple twist of his hand to the mirror body brought it into alignment. The doors and hoods were then mated with the cars and fit was

Ferrari factory, Maranello, 1989
After bolting the engine in place on one F40, worker Claudio Miglioli traveled to the far end of the assembly line to do a completely different job. With the rear canopy mounted in a special jig, he glued the Plexiglas rear window in place and laid the weather stripping around the seam. In the background, the V–8 car line was visible, with a finished F40 parked in a spare place waiting to be moved outdoors to a storage area. The car still lacked its front lights owing to a tardy supplier.

Ferrari factory, Maranello, 1989
The rear window was the first component added to the body at the start of the line; the rear side windows were some of the last parts assembled here at the end of the line. A worker used a scrap of flowered cloth to clean away excess adhesive from the weather stripping on car number 233. Stacked in the stand behind the car were F40 noses.

checked. Seams and joints were eyeballed and latches were snapped to make certain everything worked. When the rear hood didn't close correctly, two workers made final adjustments by bending and pulling and slamming. They stepped back to curse and point out the problem to a third worker, who stepped forward to use his body weight to work things into place until it all fit just right.

When an F40 was finished, it was rolled off the assembly line to await one of the several blue-overalled workers racing around the factory with mechanized lifts to carry the front wheels of the car. With the V–8 road cars' production running at capacity, the forklifts were constantly busy hauling away a finished Mondial t or the first of the 348 series, and were lax on getting to the F40 line where finishing cars

didn't run on a schedule anyway. Thus, F40 assemblers rolled the cars away to sit at open spaces nearby within the factory.

In the autumn of 1989, the access roads between factory buildings at Maranello were lined by dozens of parked F40s, complete except for the headlights and driving lights, which were needed from a tardy outside supplier before the cars could be finished and tested.

Ferrari factory, Maranello, 1989
The complete staff of the 14 F40 assembly line workers were pictured with a finished car. The front lights would be added later, after they arrived from the subcontractor.

Chapter 7

Prova

250 Km/h on the Autostrada

In the early days of the factory, according to legend, Enzo Ferrari personally checked over—and even testdrove—each finished car before it left the Maranello gates bound for a customer. From his office window, Ferrari could look out into the factory courtyard and onto the final preparations made to the car. When the car was ready, he was called outside to approve it, the anxious mechanics and workers standing behind lest he find the note of the engine noise or the paint finish not up to his exacting demands.

Such personal attention to each of his finished products may have been possible in the days of the Tipo 166, when only two or three cars

Ferrari factory, Maranello, 1989
An artist was at work within the Ferrari finishing department. This 308 GTB sat under the bright overhead lines of fluorescent bulbs that aided workers in spotting even the most minute flaws in the fit or finish of the car bodies. Rubber-headed mallets were used to fine-tune the fit of sunroofs, headlamps, doors and so on. The paint finish required more time-consuming work. Upon entrance to the shop, the cars were examined for paint imperfections and white grease pencils were used to outline the blemishes. Defects that could be buffed or polished out were fixed; others requiring repainting were sanded down, masked and sent to the paint booth. Tiny paint chips were often filled in with artist's paintbrushes and a deft hand.

were completed each month. In the era of the 250 GT series, when the assembly lines were building cars at a rate of one per day, the job of quality control would have been full-time.

In 1989, components were checked for quality before they were assembled all along the production process. Exhaustive spot-testing of one engine block in ten assured the casting was solid for a run; if a fault was discovered within the test block, the remaining blocks were all pulled for testing. Specialized workers spent their days with computers analyzing the metallurgical make-up of the alloys hand-mixed within the foundry. X-ray and magnafluxing machines were used to ensure the quality of the crankshafts. Other workers measured and miked out the tolerances on camshaft lobes, cylinder bores and so on. In the finishing shop, special lights were used to spot defects in the paint or subtle dents in the bodywork that were invisible to the unaided eye. The most glamorous quality control work was that of the test drivers.

Ferrari factory, Maranello, 1989
An auto transporter from the German importer waited to clear driving papers before leaving the rear gates with a load of new Ferraris. For transportation, Styrofoam panels were taped to the sides of the cars to protect against minor dings or scratches to the bodywork.

Ferrari factory, Maranello, 1989
The service department neighbored the finishing shop. Cars were tested in three stages, returning to the service shop in between for any alterations or to simply double-check that all was functioning properly. Here, an F40 awaited its next test drive while the lights were checked on a Testarossa.

The *prova* license plate

It was part of the Ferrari legend that the cars were tested on the neighboring roads and nearby autostrade. Stories told of 300 km/h runs along the A1 from Modena to Milan to prove prototypes. Other stories told of the meeting between the latest Ferrari and the new Iso Grifo; how the test drivers raced until one driver's car broke down, and the other driver pulled to a halt and offered a ride back to the loser's factory gates.

Legend, yes, but there was nothing like rounding a tight blind corner lined by stone farmhouses in the Emilian countryside and coming face to face with a fast, sideways Ferrari F40. Even while

150

fighting to regain control of their Fiats or bicycles as the *prova* car disappeared in the other direction, no one seemed to wave a fist in anger; instead, they swung their heads to watch. Even the *carabinieri* and *polizie* turned a blind eye to the speeds—and opened the other eye wide to assess the new designwork. The *prova* plate allowed unlimited speed by Italian law.

Coming off the assembly line at Maranello in 1989, the finished Ferrari was put in the hands of the test driver. The job of testdriving the cars was a respected one; compared with the factory line workers tied to their spots within the assembly buildings, the test drivers were like cowboys free to roam. And while the factory workers wore the

Ferrari factory, Maranello, 1989
A yellow Testarossa returned to the factory's rear gates following one of the three testing runs. All test cars exited through the rear gate, usually leaving within the first working hours in the morning and returning before the noontime meal, or leaving directly after lunch and returning before the workday was finished. Note the *prova* license plate hung on a string from the trunk of the car so it could be easily switched between test cars throughout the day. In the early days of Ferrari, the *prova* license plate was usually painted onto the tail of race cars during road tests—and often left in place through races.

Ferrari factory, Maranello, 1989
At the small paint booth in the center of the finishing department, a paint flaw on the roof of a car was resprayed. The extensive and thorough masking job protected the rest of the car's finish. Bake lights aided in drying the paint.

Ferrari blue coveralls, test drivers had no official uniform. They did have an unofficial uniform, however: stylish American blue jeans, bright polo shirts and Ray-Ban sunglasses.

The famous provisional *prova* test license plate was hung by string from the back end of the car, and the driver collected the build orders from atop the dashboard to begin the run-down of the car and its fine-tuning. The seats were covered in plastic to protect the hide or, in the case of the F40, the red cloth upholstery. With a twist of the key, the car burst into life for its maiden trip. This was not the engine's first time being started, as it had run on the dynamometer for four hours, but it was the first time the assembled car had been fired up.

With little regard for the tight new engine, the driver aimed the car for the back gate of the factory exiting onto via Musso. At the gate, a security guard checked the test papers, noting the time of departure, before lifting the gate for the car to roll past. Often, well-wishers in the form of tourists, local children and the Ferrari faithful waited to see the latest car and snap a photograph. Turning right onto via Musso, the driver revved the engine to loosen it and bring it up to temperature before turning left on the Strada vicinale del Trebbo, heading north for Modena or the autostrade. Other drivers turned left onto via Musso, turned left again onto via Abetone Inferiore, roared past the factory's main gates and zoomed through town to the south.

There were several favored routes for the test runs. For high-speed testing, cars were wrung out along the A1 autostrada, giving drivers the chance to race them up over the 200 km/h, or 124 mph, mark without much traffic interference; the route from Modena to Milan on the A1 Autostrada del Sole was straight and fast. The trip north and then south on the A15 to La Spezia or south to Bologna and over the Raticosa pass through the Apennines to Florence included numerous quick corners and twisting stretches of road. Other favored routes stayed on the rural roads surrounding Maranello, with a fine assortment of straightaways, fast curves and switchbacks running up into the mountains.

Few production cars were tested on Ferrari's test track at Fiorano. The track was used primarily for the Formula One cars and the other rare racers, such as the F40 Le Mans. Fiorano was also utilized for prototype development work by the factory, although often the cars were tested at more private tracks to hide them from spying eyes. At times, the Fiat test track at Mirafiori or the Alfa track at Balocco was used, and the prototype Testarossa was tested by Ferrari and Pininfarina on the secluded eight-mile circular Nardo racetrack at the other end of Italy, near Brindisi.

Three-stage testing

Enzo Ferrari loved the testing of his race cars. Days were spent at the famous Modena *autodromo* fine-tuning and modifying the racers for handling, power and speed. In his July 7, 1960, acceptance speech for the University of Bologna's honorary degree in mechanical engi-

Ferrari factory, Maranello, 1989
Once the car's fit and finish had been cleared, a final wax and polish was performed. Using electric buffers, a worker went over the black paint of this Testarossa.

Ferrari factory, Maranello, 1989
Following the final road test, cars were cleaned of their accumulated road grime at a makeshift wash stand within the rear gates of the factory. A Testarossa drove through the body wash while a test driver rinsed down the engine bay of a 328 GTS. The body wash relied strictly on sprayed water to clean the car; no automated brushes were used on the bodywork.

neering, Ferrari explained how his cars were built and described the testing of race cars as "the most delicate, the most engrossing and the most dramatic phase."

The day-to-day testing of the road cars, on the other hand, was routine work. Everything from temperature gauges to door handles was checked to make certain all components functioned correctly. Alongside the rear gate within the factory walls rested two metal ramps aiming into the air at approximately a 30 degree angle. Cars were run up the ramp and stopped, the parking brake set; if a car stayed put, it passed the test. In another part of the factory where finished cars waited to be delivered, a circle had been painted on the pavement. A test driver raced a 348 around the circle in dizzy, ever-tightening turns, locking up the brakes and roaring around again to test steering and braking.

All in all, each production car was run by the factory test drivers for a total of between 100 and 150 kilometers. The road tests were run in three stages, with the car returning to the service department at the factory after each pass.

The service department was in a cavernous building, painted a sterile white inside. The service workers wore red Ferrari coveralls; bending over the rear of the cars to fine-tune the engines, they looked like doctors operating on patients, their medical bags being red work chests filled with tools. Lines of test cars were slotted along the walls with mats over the bodies for the mechanics to lean on. The cars were an array of the models in production in 1989: Testarossas, Mondials and F40s, the last of the 208 GTBs, 328 GTBs, 400s and the first of the 348s.

When a car was ready for the road again, the test driver was called back. He jumped into the car, drove to the exit door, rolled down the window and reached for a long rope. He tugged the rope for the door to open, exited, tugged the rope again for the door to close, and directed the car to the rear gate and back onto the road.

When the final test was complete, the test driver chauffeured the car to a small car wash built in a Quonset hut within the factory walls neighboring the paint shop. The car was run through the sprayers inside the wash—no brushes or mechanical rollers were used on the bodywork. The car was then parked alongside the hut, where the test driver uncoiled a hose, lifted the rear hood and washed down the engine. As a fellow test driver in a Testarossa rounded the building headed for the rear gate and open road, the engine washer armed with the hose sprayed him down.

Finishing shop: Artist's paintbrushes and polish

The Ferrari finishing shop was situated next to the service shop, and like the service shop, it was spotless. Cars were parked in all directions within the shop, and workers hovered around them, each maneuvering behind himself or herself a small wheeled table bearing tools: grease pencils, artist's paintbrushes, cans of paint, rags, fine-grain sandpaper, buffers, flat-faced metalworking hammers, files and so on.

While the test drivers were usually men, most of the workers in the finishing department were women. Wearing meticulous blue Ferrari smocks, they examined the cars parked beneath rows of brilliant white overhead lights hung only feet above the vehicles' roofs. Under the lights' glow, the work area was more than balmy.

The special lights allowed the workers to spot imperfections in a car's finish. Armed with a white grease pencil, they swarmed around the cars, circling spots on the paintwork that appeared flawless to the outside eye. When they were finished, the cars looked like sides of beef marked up for the butcher's knife.

Bodyworkers then stepped in. The first stage was to attempt to buff out the imperfections with an electric buffer run carefully over each spot. If that failed, the buffer was traded for sandpaper, and the flaw was rubbed down and marked for repainting.

A glass-walled paint booth sat in the center of the finishing shop, complete with vent fans and bake lights. The offending spots on the car were masked off and resprayed. When dry, the cars were returned to the special bank of lights for double checking.

For final touchup work, an artist's paintbrush was used. With the top of a paint can as a pallet, a worker dabbed minute dots of color onto the edges of headlamp covers, hood vents or wheel arches. The workers bent over until almost touching the car with their noses, checking for the last small flaw.

Other workers used metalworking hammers to tap the edges of sunroofs and hoods to perfect the fit. Doors were opened and closed again and again, a last dab of grease added to the hinges.

When a car had passed inspection, the body was waxed, buffed and polished. Finally the vehicle was lined up by a loading dock to await a car transporter from a Ferrari concessionaire or importer, or it was parked in a holding area behind the finishing shop. Here, lines of cars sat patiently beneath the shelter of concrete parking ports. Completed F40s gathered dust alongside what appeared to be a forgotten 400 i with its battery being recharged. The rag top of a Mondial was covered in plastic, the fenders and bumpers were taped with chunks of Styrofoam for shipping protection. Testarossas with build orders still resting atop the dash shared slots with the last 328 GTS cars, marked for

Ferrari factory, Maranello, 1989
Outside the rear door of the finishing department was located a parking lot for finished cars. Ferraris from the last 412 constructed to numerous 308 and 208 GTB series cars waited for delivery or for owners to pick them up. Numerous F40s were parked under concrete ports, gathering dirt and dust from the rain. The Mondial Cabriolet at center was covered by plastic to protect the soft convertible roof. The building housing the Bar Gianni outside the factory walls was visible at center.

delivery to South Africa, Japan, the United States and other destinations. In the summer, huge sun screen nets were hoisted above the parking lot to protect paintwork.

Surrounded by the finished cars in the parking lot, a lone worker attacked a bare 348 chassis with an electric saw. The chassis had failed to pass muster before receiving its undercoating; the worker was cutting it up for scrap.

Chapter 8

The Race Shop
Ferrari's *Raison d'être*

In the beginning, all of Ferrari was the race shop. The garage and works at viale Trento e Trieste, 11 in Modena set the stage for the subsequent Reparto Corse within the walls at Maranello and the new GES, or Gestione Sportiva, based on viale Alberto Ascari, neighboring the test track. Only in later years did the Ferrari race shop become separate from the Ferrari road car production lines.

Chronicling the split between the race works and the road cars provides insight into the operations at Maranello. The division was gradual but ever growing, to the point in 1982 when it became physical as well as philosophical.

Ferrari race shop, Maranello, 1956
A view down the length of the race shop gave a good idea of the size of the works in 1956. Two *monoposti* Formula cars stood in the foreground with two sports racers being prepared in the background. Worktables lined the outside wall where the best natural light was available. *Jesse Alexander*

One of the first Ferraris to venture to the United States at the behest of Luigi Chinetti was this 4.5 liter Tipo 375 Indianapolis 500 racer of 1952. Alberto Ascari drove this car, the Ferrari Special, number 12.

Distinction between race and road cars
When Ferrari set up shop in Maranello following World War II, cars were built in the wing of the triangular factory bordering Enzo Ferrari's office, with a separate room set off to the side for engine assembly. In photographs, the inside of the workshop was austere and neat—all business with no unnecessary frills. The shop was much larger than Scaglietti's complete works at the time. Tall white walls stretched to a high ceiling and numerous large windows provided ample light for the fine work. The cars under construction were set up on metal tube stands as fine as the chassis tubework of the cars themselves. There was plenty of space to move around the cars, and worktables lined the outside wall with tools and vises for building subcomponents or fine-tuning parts. Aluminum alloy body panels hung from the walls.

In 1951–52, construction of race and road cars was placed in separate wings of the Maranello factory. For the first time since the founding of the company, two types of cars were now being built at Ferrari: the race cars for Scuderia Ferrari, the factory team, and cars for customers, whether road cars or privateer racers. Their destinations distinguished where and how the cars were built. Race cars were fabricated and assembled within the race shop; road cars were built on an "assembly line." Still, the two were separated by only a wall.

Ferrari race shop, Maranello, 1952
Dynamometer testing was performed on a V–12 engine, although it is difficult to identify the type. The dynamometer workers appeared to be hooking up the fuel lines to triple dual-throat Weber carburetors. The engines were run off the ignition coils mounted on the test bed stand. At right in glasses and dark coat, Luigi Bazzi oversaw a project surrounded by several race shop workers. Note the old-style overalls with zippered fronts and the Ferrari name written above the chest pocket. At far left, what appeared to be a Tipo 125 engine rested against the wall. *Road & Track*

This distinction between cars grew through the years as Ferrari Automobili grew. As of 1952, Ferrari was constructing more race cars than road cars by a large percentage; by the end of the 1950s, the production numbers had reversed dramatically. The road cars had also become much more strictly road cars by 1960, with pretensions of sporting luxury versus out-and-out racing muscle. In terms of technol-

ogy, components and construction techniques, the road cars also shared less with the race cars. In 1950, the difference between Ferrari race cars, with even serial numbers, and road cars, with odd serial numbers, was more modest.

When the first true production line was set up within the factory in 1960 to produce the 250 GT series cars, the race shop appeared even more old-fashioned in comparison. More than a wall within the factory now separated the two operations, but they were still within adjoining buildings. Workers were assembling more than one 250 GT road car each day, whereas in the race shop total production for the year was a mere handful.

The purchase deal struck between Enzo Ferrari and Gianni Agnelli in 1969 set the direction for both road car production and the race shop. Fiat gained control over the production lines, and over the next years injected large amounts of capital and mass-production expertise into modernizing them. Enzo Ferrari, in turn, gained the needed capital to continue running his race shop as he had in 1950.

In 1982, the new headquarters for the renamed Gestione Sportiva was opened on viale Alberto Ascari. The race shop and the road car assembly shop were now almost a half-kilometer away, within separate walls. While the factory was still in Maranello, the race shop and test track were now within the borders of the neighboring town of Fiorano. As Italian journalist Rancati stated, it was "an infinite distance nonetheless." And the physical distance would grow in philosophical and technological distance in the coming years.

Ferrari's Holy of Holies

Only rare glimpses have been allowed the outside world into the Holy of Holies that is the Ferrari race shop. Like the deepest vaults of the Vatican, the race shop has been the company's guarded secret, its arcane department whose inner workings have been hidden from the secular world. Stories abound of Ferrari racers and friends who, during rare tours of the race works, had the film removed from their cameras

---

The Chamber of Horrors

Everyone knows of the spoils of the wars—the trophies, plaques and photographs of the winning Ferraris and their drivers. Through the years, the victories were celebrated. The defeats were not.

Enzo Ferrari was not one to rest on his laurels; going racing meant winning races.

Lining a wall in the otherwise sparse offices at Maranello was a series of wood and glass cabinets that told of the losses in a reference library of Ferrari defeat. Inside Ferrari, the cabinets were infamous, nicknamed *Il museo degli errori*—The Museum of Errors. On the shelves within the cabinets lay the soiled and oxidized culprits, the offending components that lost the races through mechanical failure: connecting rods twisted like taffy, crankshafts cracked in two, holed and burned pistons, mangled valves, suspension arms that let go, cross sections of bald tires, sizzled clutches and the rest of the minor components that stopped a race in its tracks. All bore labels detailing the time, the place and the race they lost.

The other culprits were the Ferrari engineers and mechanics who designed, fabricated or prepared the components and race cars. Following the defeats, the technical postmortem was held with the offending component on the table and the personnel on the stand. Ferrari's iron hand was well-known, and the fear and dread the engineers and mechanics must have had within their stomachs entering into the postmortem can only be imagined.

---

with an almost superstitious verve, as if the spirits of the cars—not to mention any racing tricks—would be stolen by the lens.

Even those allowed inside have rarely seen anything of import. Before tours or visits, the race shop was religiously cleaned of dust on the floor as well as incriminating hardware. In 1989, during a coffee break at the Bar Gianni next door to the factory entrance on via Abetone, one race shop mechanic explained how well guarded the race shop's inner workings were. It was not only impossible to be allowed in the race shop when Ferrari was losing races, it was impossible to even

Ferrari race shop, Maranello, 1952
The race shop mechanic was dwarfed behind this early inline four-cylinder Tipo 500 Formula Two double overhead cam engine set up on the dynamometer. Note the massive bodies of the sidedraft Weber carburetors. The test bed looked to be newly erected, as several gauges were not yet in place in their mounting boards. *Road & Track*

Carrozzeria Scaglietti, Modena, 1958
Racers were sometimes bodied within the Ferrari race shop for secrecy's sake, with a panelbeater from Scaglietti making the trip south from Modena to do the metal forming. At other times, however, race cars were sent to the Scaglietti works for bodies or to be repaired, as with this early rare V–6 Dino engined sports racer. The car had been crashed and was in the shop so the front end could be rebodied. *Mark Wallach*

be allowed in the gates when Ferrari was winning. Said the mechanic: "They don't let anybody in to see the Gestione Sportiva—especially now because Ferrari is winning in Formula One. Once, several years ago, they did let a well-known Italian journalist in. But even then if they let you in, they don't let you see anything anyway."

With the money and prestige riding on Formula One racing in the 1980s, Ferrari had virtually closed off the race shop. It wasn't always so. In the 1950s, Ferrari was looking for publicity—and the racing world was perhaps younger and more innocent.

In 1958, American motorsports photographer Jesse Alexander received rare permission to photograph inside the race shop. His pictures showed the sunlight pouring through the tall side windows, casting an ancient, mythical glow to the workings. In the shop rested four race cars: two Grand Prix cars and two sports racers. Two block-and-tackle hoists hung from overhead beams and welding gas tanks sat at the ready. The work space was clean, tidy and organized, yet lining the walls were an assortment of wheels and tires, old seats, car hoods, axles fixed with the monstrous drum brakes, and, in one photo, a broom and dustpan.

Alexander's photographs of the race shop contrast with other pictures he shot in the main road car assembly wing at the same time. In the race works, a Monza was being assembled, set up on tubework stands with about six workers surrounding it. Some workers were crouched on their knees beneath the body; one worker had his head in a wheelwell; other workers stood atop wooden sawhorses and bent forward into the engine bay. On the single-runway assembly line in the

road car works, 250 GTs were being constructed. With the cars at head-height, bolting together the undercarriage was easy; walkways along the line were lowered slightly from the cars, allowing access to the engines without sawhorses or sore backs. Much thought and planning had gone into the ergonomics of working on the road car assembly line, while the race cars were built as they always had been and the race works saved ergonomics for the car's cockpit and driver.

American Mark Wallach visited the race shop in 1958 with a technical eye, as he was racing Ferraris at Le Mans. Wallach also had a photographic eye trained upon the works—until the film was unrolled from his camera.

Wallach's most vivid remembrance was of the crashed and burned Grand Prix cars scattered throughout the shop. Visiting on a Saturday evening, he was amazed by the around-the-clock activity on a weekend. Workers were bent over the racers, scavenging salvageable components and throwing the rest out. Other workers took a ruined Formula One parts car, sawed it in half and welded a section onto another car that was being set up for the next race. "It's no wonder today's historians have such a difficult time tracking down the serial numbers on the race cars," Wallach said. "This was not the General Motors assembly plant at all."

Day-to-day workings inside the race shop

New Zealander Bob Wallace worked within the Ferrari race shop on and off in 1961 and 1962 before leaving to work at Lamborghini for the next twelve years. He remembered some of the day-to-day workings inside the race shop.

In the early 1960s, Ferrari's racing effort was at its peak, challenging the world with Grand Prix cars, prototypes, sports racers and homologated production cars, from the shark-nosed Formula One Tipo 156F1, 250 GT Tour de France and the last days of the Testa Rossa in 330 guise as the TRI/62 to the dawn of the new generation of Scuderia Ferrari racers, the first SP cars, the 250 GTO, the 250 LM and the great P cars. The concessionaires and privateers were also at their zenith, including Luigi Chinetti's NART, Colonel Ronnie Hoare's Maranello Concessionaires, Georges Filipinetti's Swiss *scuderia,* the Belgian Ecurie Francorchamps, French importer Charles Pozzi, Scuderia Serenissima and others. Thus, the Maranello race shop was a blurr of activity, through long nights, with a multitude of people hovering over the cars and the Scuderia drivers milling around the periphery.

Wallace recalled: "Old Ferrari was racing every damn sort of car there was at the time. He didn't care about the customers or the road cars—they were just one way to help pay for the race cars. He sold off the old race cars and extra race cars to the customers to make more money, and he was racing in all these different categories to win as much as possible and try to make the race cars at least contribute to the costs they incurred."

The race shop employed some thirty workers full-time, and a dozen of those traveled with the cars to each outing. The race works had its own complete line of machine tools so as not to be dependent on the main assembly sector and its more regular hours. For emergencies, the race shop even employed a nighttime machinist. Wallace continued: "In the race shop, we had a philosophy to try to make as much

Ferrari race shop, Maranello, 1956
Early on in the construction, a sports racer with the tubework chassis was set atop stands for working on. A Tipo 410 Sport waited in the background.

Panelbeating dollies were mounted on stands against the wall. *Jesse Alexander*

of the basic car ourselves—build the chassis, the engines, the whole thing."

At that time, even with the first assembly line up and running at Ferrari, the race shop and the road car production were tightly linked in terms of both technology and personnel. Wallace: "The race department at Maranello was an integral part of the whole factory. It was only one wing, but it was always connected to the rest.

"The relationship between the two was close. There was not enough personnel to do work in just the race shop or just the production lines, and so the two were connected here as well. The engineering personnel could be at work in the race shop and a problem would come

up and they would be called next door to the assembly lines to solve it, and vice versa."

Race shop technical director Mauro Forghieri recounted the relationship between the race and road car engineering at the same time period. Forghieri and associates were working on both street and track cars simultaneously, as he stated in an interview with Dutch journalist Wim Oude Weernink for *Automobile Quarterly*.

Forghieri: "In the Fifties, all Ferraris were competition cars more or less. But with the Super America and Europa GT, we started to build pure road cars with detuned competition engines. This led to exciting cars like the 250 GT and GTE. The technical racing department was in

charge of designing some special road cars that led to the 250 Lusso, the 275 GTB and the Daytona."

Still, even with the close race shop/road car assembly line relationship, there was a definite class structure within the factory, a hierarchy that remained in place into the 1990s. Most workers were employed on the production car side of the company, working in the foundry, finishing castings, building components and assembling cars. Those who assembled the engines for the road cars were a step up; most had been through the Ferrari mechanics school or had received similar training. Above all were the race shop workers.

Wallace: "Most workers stayed in one place, but depending on circumstances and necessity, they could be moved around. Department heads always kept a watch out. If they found an exceptionally good worker, he could get bumped over to build race cars next door. On the other hand, if you messed something up in the race shop, you could find yourself bolting rear ends on cars on the assembly line."

With the high level of activity on so many racing fronts, work in the race shop was strenuous and tiring—win or lose. Long hours were the norm. Wallace: "Old Ferrari ruled the factory damn near like a feudal kingdom. He knew what he wanted to do and how to do it, and that was the way things went. But everyone was treated very well. Ferrari could be an extremely hard man, but he was always very just and fair.

"I remember one time working in the race shop. It was midnight or some crazy hour—that sort of thing—Old Ferrari came by to see how things were progressing. He saw us working there and he ordered the department heads to have some hot dinner made for us and find a car to drive us home, saying that we were all too tired to go on that night."

That spirit left an indelible impression on Bob Wallace. Like Phil Hill before him, he was struck by the vitality of the race shop—and the factory in general. Racing has always been the raison d'être for Ferrari, and workers have always rooted for their *equipe,* whether they worked in the race shop or on the assembly line. As one road car engine builder said in 1989, "We are all Ferraristi. Naturally I am a Formula One *apassionato.*"

As Wallace remembered, "There was a lot of pride at Ferrari, lots of enthusiasm. Anyone who worked there felt it, from the workers in the foundry to the front gatekeeper. The average person was proud to be at Ferrari, proud of what they were doing and how they did it. That pride has passed down to today—never mind the political parties, the unions, the strikes and so on. Today, Ferrari is completely different. But the spirit is still there."

Ferrari race shop, Maranello, 1956
A Tipo 290 MM was built atop stands in the race shop. Five mechanics were at work on the car, perhaps in a rush before a race. Crouching down underneath the car or standing bent over on wooden sawhorses would probably have meant sore backs at the end of the workday. The aluminum bodywork had been formed at Scaglietti and transferred to the race shop where the engine, driveline and mechanicals were assembled. *Jesse Alexander*

At Work in the Race Shop: Upholstering the 250 GTO

Legend, from the remembrances of Ermanno and Romano Luppi, former Ferrari race shop workers and, as of 1989, Ferrari upholstery restorers based in Modena:

While the workers on the assembly lines building road cars punched the time clock with regular weekly hours, mechanics in the race shop stayed late, often laboring through the night and weekends to build or prep a car for an upcoming race. The prototype 250 GTO serial number 3223 GT was constructed in this way within the race shop at Maranello in 1962.

The 250 GTO chassis and engine—and even the electrics—were everyday workings for the mechanics. The aerodynamic bodywork was special and revolutionary, but still within the realm of the seasoned race car builders. Upholstery of the seats, however, was a minor detail, often left to the last.

The last minute for the 250 GTO prototype's upholstery came sometime after midnight, and the factory's store was closed. With the car destined for testing or to come before Enzo Ferrari's inspection first thing in the morning, the seats needed finishing.

The workers frantically searched the race shop for upholstery material. The only cloth available was a nice clean set of brilliant medium blue Ferrari cotton coveralls, the famous uniform of the factory workers. Whether the coveralls came off the back of a mechanic or were just an extra set isn't clear, but the fabric was cut to fit and sewn in place.

The story may be only a story. The truth is that many Ferrari factory sports racers of the 1960s from the 250 GTO through to the 250 LM and other sports racers had seats upholstered in brilliant medium blue cotton fabric.

Building the 1969 Tipo 312F1

On June 5, 1969, the British magazine *Autocar* reported on the Ferrari race shop—just before Fiat's partial purchase of Ferrari. Journalist Edward Eves described in detail how the 1969 Tipo 312F1 cars were constructed.

Once the design had been set, the centerlines of the car were laid out on a large worktable central to the race shop and the tube frame was tack-welded together. Bulkheads made from tubes and sheet metal were fabricated and then added to the framework. The instrument panel was cut from light-gauge sheet metal, perforated to hold the gauges and tack-welded in place. A dummy engine was then hoisted into the chassis by a crane so motor mounts and component brackets could be sized, fabricated, fitted and welded in place; for, as Eves wrote,

Ferrari race shop, Maranello, 1956

A Ferrari-Lancia Formula One racer was prepared for action: the engine was a V-8 Lancia but the bodywork said Ferrari. Spare nuts and bolts were stored at hand in half an Esso tin, resting atop the filters of the carburetor velocity stacks. In the background were the extra seats and the side panniers for the race car, at left. *Jesse Alexander*

"it is unlikely that drawings of every bracket will have been made"—an insight into the structural design work the mechanics performed on the job.

"There's lots of interesting detail work visible at this stage which is later hidden," Eves observed, commenting in particular on the use of wooden strips set into the U-section frame ribs surrounding the fuel cell. The wood was to prevent chafing of the bag on the metal, and the frame tubes and body panel rivets were also inspected for any protrusions that could harm the fuel cell.

To support and not stress the body panels, outriggers were run from the main suspension tubes to the skin. "Ferrari never throws a good idea away," Eves wrote. The tubular construction with stressed paneling was inherited from the Lancia D50 cars given to Ferrari when Vincenzo Lancia made his exit from Formula One racing in 1955. It was much like Touring's Superleggera construction as well, using light alloy body panels attached to the frame tubes with pop rivets. The panels were made in the race shop where Scaglietti had a small team for the confidential race work. Fiberglass nose fairings and cockpit covers completed the aluminum-bodied chassis.

Meanwhile, the 312F1 V–12 engine was built in the assembly room off the main race shop. The Electron engine blocks and sumps were specially cast in a corner of the factory's regular foundry; the fine machining was performed in the race shop. The crankshaft was machined from a billet of nickel-chrome-steel on a Boehringer lathe, an operation requiring some eighty-four hours. H-section racing connecting rods were also machined from solid blanks. The cast cylinder liners and diecast light alloy pistons came from Borgo. The assembled engine was then bench-tested on the race shop's dynamometer.

A Borg and Beck two-plate clutch transmitted power to the gearbox. Eves reported that until 1967, Ferrari fabricated its own racing clutches—an amazing amount of work for such a small-scale race shop. Eves also commented on the beautiful work that went into the ball-bearing-spline transmission halfshafts, individually machined from billets.

The suspension showed evidence of further fine artisanship. The suspension arms were built of welded tubes for lightness, and the swinging top link was built up by welding together sheet steel and machined forgings. Time-consuming work.

A return to Scuderia Ferrari

In 1981, Italian journalist Gianni Cancellieri, editor of *Autosprint,* visited the Ferrari race shop. This tour chronicled the last year the Gestione Sportiva was headquartered within the factory walls before the vast new works was built in Maranello in 1982.

Cancellieri's visit came just days after Gilles Villeneuve's underdog victory at Monte Carlo in the turbocharged Tipo 126CK Formula One car, and the race shop was still in high spirits. As Cancellieri

Ferrari race shop, Maranello, 1956

A Tipo 500 TR inline four-cylinder engine was tested on the race shop dynamometer between runs. Note the gauges mounted on the board and the key on a chain to switch the assembly on. Around the test bed sat the usual parts and equipment: a spare transmission resting against the left wall, tubing and canisters of Shell X–100 motor oil against the right. *Jesse Alexander* wrote: "Today is Friday, but here at the 'Gestione Sportiva' . . . it is just another day. By now the Monte Carlo victory has been filed away and when spoken about the tone of voice is detached, as if it were just one of the thousand pieces forming a vast puzzle of creative experience acquired over so many years around all the world's race tracks. A rampant horse flag is hoisted in the bodywork assembly shop. 'It is tradition,' I am assured by [Franco] Gozzi who is in charge of press relations and a real 'Richelieu' at the court of King Enzo—'It is done each time we win, I'm not just saying that.' "

Cancellieri detailed the layout of the race works, giving a picture of its small size and the vast amount of work performed within. The long main room looked like a corridor, with additional rooms partitioned off by metal-and-glass walls. Separate rooms accommodated a gearbox assembly shop, electronics shop, engine assembly room and the engine test room equipped with no less than five dynamometer test beds. Cancellieri described the last room as "a kind of *sancta sanctorum,*" where the high priest was the engine tester, "confessing" a 126CX that would run at the next Grand Prix in Jarama, Spain. "The poor sinner, the engine, cannot lie," wrote Cancellieri; horsepower, torque, turbocharger atmospheric pressure and more were all registered, noted and adjusted as the engine was wrung of its secrets. Perhaps it would be more accurate to compare the engine tester to a high inquisitor with a torture rack.

Cancellieri also visited the race shop technical office, a vast room of desks divided by glass partitions. Here were the tables and drawing boards of the designers, all "collaborators" of race department chief Mauro Forghieri, who sat in a far corner, "talking and gesticulating."

The picture that emerged from Cancellieri's report was fascinating. The race shop as of 1981 was a complete factory-within-the-factory, different from the race-shop-integral-with-the-factory that

Help from Customer Service: The 365 GTB/4 Comp.

When the 365 GTB/4 Daytona was unveiled as a road car in 1969, Ferrari race privateers saw its possibilities for racing. At this period, Ferrari had not built a production racer since the 250 LM of 1963–65 and had pulled out of GT racing in 1964. The race teams petitioned Ferrari for a competition version of the production Daytona. Ferrari, finally, agreed.

The 365 GTB/4 was never designed as a race car. It was the last V–12 front-engined two-passenger Ferrari in the new era heralded by the mid-engined Lamborghini Miura road car. The 365 GTB/4 was constructed on the Maranello assembly lines alongside the 246 GT, bodied by Scaglietti with panels from Pininfarina. To convert production cars to race specs, engine tuning, lightweight body panels and suspension modifications would be required. All in all, substantial work.

The factory chose not to do the conversion work within the race shop or as a special series built on the assembly lines. Nevertheless, the days of the small-run special series cars were not finished at Ferrari. Sixteen

Ferrari customer service shop, Modena, 1972
The modern customer service shop was built at viale 11 Trento e Trieste in Modena after the old Scuderia Ferrari building was razed. Cars and parts could be ordered here, and service was performed in the garages; an inner courtyard provided parking for customer cars. The Ferrari customer service shop and several subcontractors in the area constructed the 365 GTB/4 Daytona Comp. cars from 1971 to 1973, followed by the 365 GT4 BB Comp. models beginning in 1971. *Hilary A. Raab, Jr.*

365 GTB/4 Comp. Daytonas were built from 1969 to 1973 in the new Ferrari Customer Service shop at viale Trento e Trieste, 11 in Modena.

Ferrari may have had several reasons for this choice. First, the cars were to be specials in an era when the assembly lines were coming under the direction of Fiat, and such a special would have disrupted the companies' designs on mass production. Second and probably more important, Enzo Ferrari had no plans to, and in fact never did, race the 365 GTB/4 with the factory team. Thus, the Comp. cars would be built as customer-request specials, foreshadowing at least in spirit the later 288 GTO and F40.

The first 365 GTB/4 Comp. Daytona was a special among the later Comp. specials. Serial number 12547 was modified by the factory at the behest of Luigi Chinetti in 1969. There is disagreement concerning where this car was built—Maranello or Customer Service, although the reasons given for constructing the cars in Modena would seem to hold true for this first out-of-series car as well. The car was essentially stock except for a lightweight aluminum body, and Chinetti reportedly picked it up and drove it to Le Mans on the night before practice for the endurance race began.

From 1971 to 1973, Customer Service built fifteen additional Comp. cars in three series of five cars each, based on the modifications made to the 12547 car. The first-series cars were based on stock chassis fitted with lightweight aluminum and fiberglass bodies, roll bars, air dams and Plexiglas side windows. The stock engine was tuned on the first-series cars, but the second- and third-series cars received modified engines with higher-lift cams, ported and polished heads, and other competition conversions, boosting horsepower to some 400 bhp on the second series and 450 bhp on the final cars. Racing tires and progressively wider wheels and antiroll bars were fitted throughout the three series.

Surprisingly, the 365 GTB/4 Comp. cars were not the last race cars to be built by Ferrari Customer Service in Modena. With the arrival of the 365 GT4 BB in 1971, privateers from Luigi Chinetti and NART to Charles Pozzi in France saw the same possibilities as with the Daytona. Again the Berlinetta Boxer was conceived as a road car and again substantial conversion was needed to bring it up to race specs. And again the work was done at Customer Service.

Ferrari race shop, Maranello, 1975
The last remnants of Ferrari's factory sports racing days were body panels from the 512 and 312PB cars stacked behind a building at the race shop. The factory quit all but Formula One racing in 1973, and as of 1989 its self-imposed ban was still in effect. *Hilary A. Raab, Jr.*

Ferrari race shop, Maranello, circa 1974
Formula One 312 T cars were constructed within the old Maranello race shop. Much as in the early days, the cars were set on tube-frame stands for assembly. Furthermore, working ergonomics did not seem to have improved substan-

tially; note the mechanic on his back underneath the car at left. As in the old race shop, tools, components and junk lined the worktables and walls. The worker at far left was apparently taking a break, sitting in the car's cockpit.
National Automotive History Collection, Detroit Public Library

Ferrari race shop, Fiorano, 1989
It was time for the noon meal, and Ferrari Formula One mechanics left by means of the Gestione Sportiva's front entrance en route to the cafeteria. The

nondescript square buildings were painted in white versus the famous Modena-yellow of the factory.

Bob Wallace worked for in 1961–62. Looked at in another way, the Gestione Sportiva was the donjon, or keep, of the grand castle that was Ferrari's feudal realm at Maranello. The race shop mirrored the Ferrari factory as a whole but in miniature with its separate technical office and drawing boards, engine and car assembly shops, and so on. The personnel in the race shop as listed by Cancellieri also reflected this: a small crew of highly specialized workers capable of fabricating the race cars almost autonomously from the factory. Thus, while Fiat had built up the assembly lines and road car production levels, here in the race shop, Enzo Ferrari had retreated to a specialty race car building shop of

the size and sophistication that he desired. A return to the early, glorious days of the prewar Scuderia Ferrari.

The Fiorano race shop and test track in the 1990s
In 1989, the race shop was off-limits; only authorized race personnel were allowed within the gates. Ferrari was a contender in Formula One with Nigel Mansell and Gerhard Berger. Alain Prost had signed for 1990.

To the outside world, the new Gestione Sportiva constructed in 1982 was a series of dull cement buildings set in a U-shape around a

171

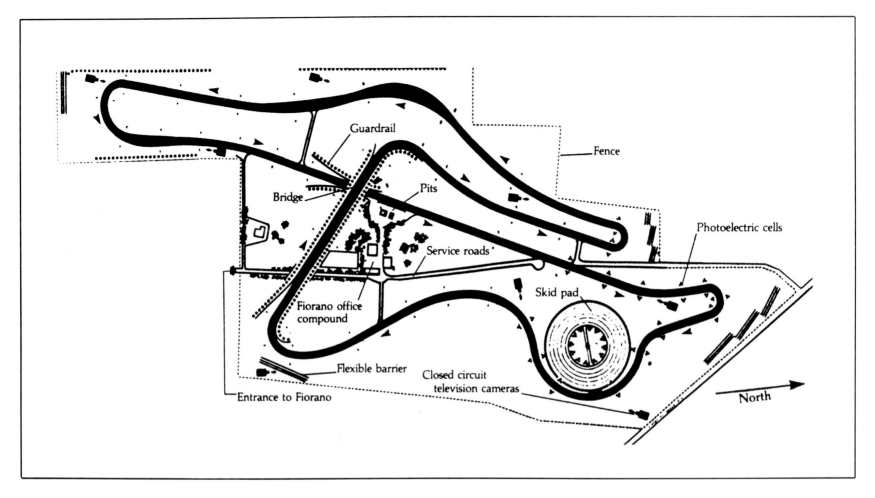

Guardrail

Fence

Bridge

Pits

Photoelectric cells

Service roads

Skid pad

Fiorano office compound

Flexible barrier

Closed circuit television cameras

North

Entrance to Fiorano

A map of the Fiorano test track as of 1990 showed the rough figure eight layout. The pits, office compound, cameras, photo cells and crash barriers were also visible. The road bordering the track on the northern end was via Abetone Inferiore, approximately one kilometer northwest from the factory. *Ferrari S.p.A.*

central courtyard at the cul-de-sac end of viale Alberto Ascari. The outside walls, curiously, were painted white instead of the Modena-yellow of the factory walls. Chain link fences surrounded the works and a slatted fence stretched across the front, broken only by a sliding, electronically controlled gate. Where the old factory race shop had been humble and unassuming, the new shop was expansive, modern, showy.

As did the race shop within the factory walls, the new shop contained a technical office and design studios, but the space was primarily given over to workshops, dynamometers and machine tools.

Ferrari test track Fiorano, 1989
This was the view of the test track most people saw. Off a dead end street behind the race shop, a path ran to the chain link fence encircling the track. Maranello schoolchildren and Ferraristi could watch the proceedings with a good view, even sneaking onto the course through the hole in the fence.

An autoclave for curing composite bodywork was constructed at the new shop by the Panini firm of Maranello. All foundry work was done at the main factory alongside the production casting lines.

Italian Gino Rancati, who had visited the early works in Modena in its heyday, was one of the first journalists to view the inside of the new race shop. His comments in *Ferrari, l'unico* were mixed: half enthusiasm and wonder at the scale of the new shop, half nostalgia for the former shop. Rancati: "It was a much larger building, plain, in square style. It was a headquarters which, when seen from the outside, gave no idea of what it contained. . . . The workshop gave the same impression [as the Maranello race shop]—it was also a gem, and was maintained like a top-class watchmaker's shop. . . . But everything had changed so much that I felt a pang in my heart. Where was the unforgettable, modest Ferrari workshop of the epic years?"

Personnel within the new Gestione Sportiva also increased with the times. Bob Wallace reported thirty workers in the factory race shop in 1961–62. The new shop boasted 194 workers in 1984. And in 1988, the number of workers to support the two Formula One drivers was 227—seven more than Scaglietti's 220.

Spectators came and went from the dead end street before the race shop, stopping for a moment in hopes of seeing the latest Formula One car rolled across the courtyard and settling instead for a snapshot of the faceless pilgrimage sight. A large rock sat by the front fence, a step up for viewers peering into the inner sanctum. A path was beaten around the perimeter of the fence: all that was visible were old wooden packing crates. A sole V–8 race engine, discarded among the crates, oxidized in a dark outside corner. The ancient adage that a two-year-old race car is junk still held true.

Ferrari was one of only a few race car makers to have their own test track when the Fiorano track was built in 1972. The track was three kilometers, or 1.86 miles, in length, designed loosely as a figure eight circuit.

Fourteen turns made up the figure eight, each modeled after a corner on a famous racetrack. What better way to test race cars than on the tracks they will be racing? Barring that, why not build one racetrack with a combination of simulated corners and straightaways from several of the toughest circuits? The same concept was used in building the first wind tunnel to test aerodynamics with simulated air speed. Thus, Fiorano had two hairpin curves—one to the left, one to the right—borrowed from those on the Monaco Grand Prix circuit, which runs the city streets. Long, sweeping fast bends mirrored the curves at Silverstone, home of the British Grand Prix, and Monza, home of the Italian Grand Prix. Elements of the old Nurburgring, Le Mans and Spa-Francorchamps circuits also appeared.

For testing the speed of cars on the track, Fiorano was posted with an intricate system of electronic timing sensors and video cameras. The curves of the track were lined by forty-four light-beam timing recorders set at intervals of forty-five meters, or 148 feet. Passing through the light beam, a car triggered the sensors, and elapsed time reports on its speed were printed out simultaneously on a computer in the Fiorano control room. The elaborate timing system was constructed for Ferrari by Longines and Olivetti.

In addition to the objective reporting of the electronic timing system, fourteen video cameras could follow a car's lap on closed circuit

Ferrari race shop, Fiorano, 1989
A wing of the race shop. The pace of work at the Gestione Sportiva was strenuous, according to one veteran race shop mechanic: "Often before a race, we all needed to be at work by six in the morning, and there is so much to do—watch out for this and that, prepare this, rebuild that—and there is no time to eat until seven at night. It's almost not worth it."

television monitors in the control room. One camera was sited at each of the fourteen corners, and engineers could assess the suspension, brakes and overall behavior of the car at speed. Formula One Ferraris could post average speeds on the Fiorano track hovering at 200 to 210 km/h, or 105 to 110 mph.

Enzo Ferrari spent some of the last years of his life in a brick house neighboring the pit and garages at the Fiorano test track alongside the race shop. There he had living quarters and a kitchen, and no longer traveled each day from Modena to the factory, or ate at the Ristorante Cavallino in Maranello.

As at the race shop, similar well-beaten paths make their ways to the chain link fence surrounding the test track. Holes have been cut in the fence, patched over and cut again; the devotion is sincere and tenacious. And when the next-generation Formula One car or production car prototype makes its rounds of the track, the fence is spotted with the faces of visiting Ferraristi and the local schoolboys and girls.

Ferrari race shop, Fiorano, 1989
Sitting between packing crates and boxes along an outside wall of the Gestione Sportiva was an old Formula One engine, covered in oil and slowly oxidizing with the elements.

Index